Illustrated by François Thisdale

What A STORY!

Angelo Georgakatos

D1503628

LES ÉDITIONS
CEC

9001, boul. Louis-H.-La Fontaine, Anjou (Québec) Canada H1J 2C5
Téléphone : 514-351-6010 • Télécopieur : 514 351-3534

Editorial Management
Carolyn Faust

Production Management
Danielle Latendresse

Production Coordination
Rodolphe Courcy

Editorial Coordination
Diane Ferland

Graphic Coordination
Louise Chabot

Rights Research
Nancy Schmidt

Cover and Page Design

Illustrator
François Thisdale

Les Éditions CEC inc. remercient le gouvernement du Québec de l'aide financière accordée à l'édition de cet ouvrage par l'entremise du Programme de crédit d'impôt pour l'édition de livres, administré par la SODEC.

Match Point, What a Story!
© 2010, Les Éditions CEC inc.
9001, boul. Louis-H.-La Fontaine
Anjou (Québec) H1J 2C5

Dépôt légal: 2010 (What a Story!)
Dépôt légal: 2012 (Competency Development and Text-Based Grammar and Short Story Pack, I Pad Version)
Bibliothèque et Archives nationales du Québec
Bibliothèque et Archives Canada

ISBN 978-2-7617-3084-6 (What a Story!)
ISBN 978-2-7617-4016-6 (Competency Development and Text-Based Grammar and Short Story Pack, I Pad Version)

Imprimé au Canada
3 4 5 6 7   16 15 14 13 12

PHOTO SOURCES

TEXT SOURCES

PP. 6–12: "Eye-Witness" by Donald S. Aitken, © 1936 by the Frank A. Munsey Co. Reprinted by permission of Argosy Communications.

P. 16: "A Poison Tree" by William Blake, public domain.

PP. 22–25: "After Twenty Years" by O. Henry, public domain.

PP. 34–37: "The Bully" by Roger Dean Kiser. Used by permission of author.

PP. 46–49: "There's a Man in the Habit of Hitting Me on the Head with an Umbrella" by Fernando Sorrentino. Translation by Clark M. Zlotchew. Used by permission of author and translator.

P. 52: "I Am Habit," Anonymous, public domain.

PP. 58–62:"The Hairpin" by Guy de Maupassant, public domain.

PP. 70–75: "Examination Day" by Henry Slesar, © Henry Slesar 1958; originally appeared in Playboy Magazine, reprinted courtesy of Ann Elmo Agency, Inc.

P. 78: "Bow Your Head" by Anonymous, public domain.

PP. 84–93: "The Last Spin" by Evan Hunter. Copyright © 1960, 1988 by Evan Hunter. Published with permission of Gelfman Schneider Literary Agents. All rights reserved.

PP. 102–105: "The Kiss" by Kate Chopin, public domain.

TABLE OF CONTENTS

FRANÇOIS THISDALE

François Thisdale is an award-winning freelance illustrator. His eye-catching style combines traditional drawing and painting with computer imagery. When François is not creating art, he's writing stories and composing music.

BORN January 8, 1964, Montréal, Québec

QUOTE "My work is my passion. It demands a lot from me, but I love it. And my reward? I'm achieving my dreams."

MORE ABOUT FRANÇOIS THISDALE

- As a child, François was always creating art. In elementary school, he entertained his friends with sketches of hockey players and comic book heroes.
- His father was a musician and his mother was an amateur painter.
- During his teenage years, both of his parents encouraged him to follow his dream of becoming an artist.
- At the age of 17, François went to CEGEP to study graphic art. Although he never worked as a graphic designer, the skills he learned there helped him to develop his artistic style.
- Over his 23-year career, François has drawn thousands of illustrations and worked for clients in Canada, the USA, France, Argentina and Korea.
- Today, he lives close to Montréal in the town of Carignan, with his wife and daughter, Nini, who he calls "a marvelous girl."

EYE-WITNESS

ABOUT THE AUTHOR

DONALD S. AITKEN

Although we've made every attempt possible to find information on Mr. Aitken, we still know very little about him. Some of the following are strictly assumptions.

BORN He was probably born in the early 20th century, since most of his published work appeared in the 1930s.

QUOTE He probably once said something like this: "Being private and mysterious makes people want to know more about you."

MORE ABOUT DONALD S. AITKEN

- He went to Australia from England at nineteen and spent four years working on cattle and sheep stations as a stockman and boundary rider.
- He later lived in New York where he wrote detective and adventure tales.
- "Murder Service" was also published for Scandinavian audiences.
- The "Eye-Witness" story was published in this weekly detective fiction magazine printed in May 1930.

RECOGNITIONS INCLUDE:

- We may assume Mr. Aitken has already received several distinctions and awards for his work, but this cannot be verified. We give him the "Most Secretive Author" award, for obvious reasons.

OTHER WORKS:

These are actual stories he has written:

- *Remedy for Death*
- *Africa Pays Her Debts*
- *Attempted Suicide*
- *The Body in the Chimney*
- *A Game for Two*
- *Jewel Robber*
- *The Last Wall*

- *A Man's Worst Enemy*
- *Murder Service*
- *Play Safe—And Die*
- *Postlude to Murder*
- *Switched Loot*
- *Thirst*

STORY SET-UP ...

In Chapter 1, you looked at how people deal with too much information. In this story, the villain's plan for revenge forces him to deal with a lot of new information. The result: overload! The success of his revenge depends upon how well he can control his emotions and manage new information at the same time. Incorrectly filtering a lot of new information sometimes leads to overload ... and oversight.

A Before Reading

ACTIVITY 1

❯ Associate the following words from the story with an appropriate antonym:

a)	noiselessly (adv.)	i)	slowly
b)	spotless (adj.)	ii)	patiently
c)	swiftly (adv.)	iii)	dull
d)	helplessly (adv.)	iv)	confidently
e)	eagerly (adv.)	v)	loudly
f)	drooping (adj.)	vi)	raised
g)	withdrawal (n.)	vii)	deposit
h)	clever (adj.)	viii)	calmness
i)	bewilderment (n.)	ix)	dirty

ACTIVITY 2

❯ Our emotions often interfere with our ability to correctly filter information and use proper judgment. In the story, a man's strong emotions and desire for revenge cause him to miss key pieces of information. Discuss the following ideas with a partner:

a) Situations/scenarios you believe may involve emotions interfering with judgment.

b) Possible consequences of letting strong emotions cloud your judgment.

c) Ideas for keeping calm and focused when your emotions begin to interfere with your judgment.

ACTIVITY 3

» In the story, you'll read about how one of the negative consequences of too much readily available information is called identity theft. What confidential information do you think thieves look for? Why?

» What can you do to make sure the confidential information you mentioned above remains confidential?

B During Reading

» Summarize the main idea or event for each of the following text parts as you read each section.

Beginning to line 38 "And now— I've come back!"	"Sweat beads …" (line 39) to "Patterson looked surprised" (line 85)	"You thought I was …" (line 86) to "Patterson sat with …" (line 108)	"When the bell …" (line 109) to "The taxi driver stood …" (line 160)	"Inside, Judd limped …" (line 161) to the end.

» As you read, note character details about Judd, Patterson and the taxi driver. What evidence supports your assumption?

Your answers may take this form:

Examples:

- Judd is (character detail) because he (evidence).

- Patterson is (character detail) because he (evidence).

- The taxi driver is (character detail) because he (evidence).

EYE-WITNESS

BY DONALD S. AITKEN

J udd eased open the screen door at the rear of the cottage and
slipped from the warm afternoon sun into the cool kitchen. He closed
the door noiselessly behind him. Then he stood perfectly still, listening.
When he caught the faint clack-clack of a typewriter in another part
005> of the house, his bearded lips spread and became an oily smile of
satisfaction. He drew an automatic from his pocket.

In the front room of the cottage a man in a spotless linen suit was
seated with his back to the door, bent over a typewriter. His fingers
moved over the keys swiftly, without hesitation. He did not hear the
010> door open. The first **intimation** that he was not alone came when
a menacing voice behind him breathed softly:

"Hello, Patterson!"

The clatter of the typewriter ceased abruptly. The man in the linen
suit froze in his **hunched-up** position. He did not look around.

015> Judd circled to the front of the desk. There was a **wariness** in his
narrowed eyes.

"No fast moves!" he warned. "This gun's **liable** to go off!"

With the two men facing each other, the effect was startling. They
were strangely alike. Each had a brown, pointed beard. Their noses
020> were long and lean. They were not old men, both looked under forty.

"Who are you?" Patterson demanded in a deep, booming voice.
His wide-open eyes did not blink.

A chuckle came from the man with the gun. "You don't recognize
me with the beard, eh? What about my voice—isn't that familiar?"

025> The man in the linen suit caught his breath sharply. Shock registered
on his face.

"Harry Judd!" he gasped.

"Yes. Harry Judd's back!" the intruder **snarled**.

Patterson's hands gripped the edge of the desk convulsively.

030> "My God!" he cried in an agonized voice. "Haven't you done enough to me? Don't you know I'm—."

"Yes, I know. You're a *cripple*. I watched you *hobbling* around in the garden just now. You've been like that, I suppose, since the day twelve years ago when I hit you over the head with a *monkey wrench* and

035> pushed you off the cliff along High Point Road. I hated you then. I intended your death to look like an accident, but by some miracle you were still alive when the searching party found you. I had to leave Penfield in a hurry. And now—I've come back!"

Sweat beads had broken out on Patterson's white face.

040> "What do you want?" His deep voice sounded choked. This man had already injured him terribly.

Judd went on. "Six months ago I came across your picture in a newspaper. It was the first I'd heard of you since I left Penfield. You've risen in the world—become

045> a successful *playwright*. You're wealthy." Grim determination came into his eyes. "I want money, Patterson. Understand? Money!"

Patterson gulped helplessly. "I don't keep

050> money in the house— there isn't twenty dollars."

"I didn't expect there would be. I want to see your bank book."

"You can't—"

055> "Shut up!" Judd made a threatening motion with the gun. "Get your bank book, I said!"

Patterson sat breathing hard for a moment. Then he reached over and opened the right hand drawer of the desk. Without lowering

Glossary

Intimation: clue; indication
hunched-up: bent with shoulders forward
wariness: watchfulness; caution
liable: at risk
snarled: growled; used an angry tone
cripple: unable to walk normally
hobbling: walking unevenly
monkey wrench: heavy tool that has two jaws
playwright: person who writes plays

060> his eyes he fumbled among some papers, finally producing a slim book secured by an elastic band. Several cancelled cheques were laid length wise in it.

Judd took the bank book eagerly, glanced into it. His **buttonhole eyes** glittered.

065> "You've done even better than I thought," he said finally. "Now listen! You're going to write a cheque for twenty-five thousand dollars, payable to yourself. Then you're going to call up the National Merchants Bank in Penfield and tell them you're coming down right away to cash it. Ask them to have the money ready. Understand?"

070> Patterson **balked**. "That's all the money I have!" he cried. "You can't force me to do this!"

Savagery swept over Judd's face.

"You see this gun, don't you? I can put a bullet through you if you refuse!" His expression softened a little. "Do as I tell you, and there's 075> nothing to be afraid of. I don't want to kill you but—" his face hardened again "I will if you drive me to it!"

Patterson **deliberated** only a moment. Then he took out his cheque book, felt for his fountain pen. He made out the cheque.

Judd compared the signature with those on the cancelled cheques.

080> "Good!" he said. "You're being **sensible**. Now phone the bank."

He held the gun close against Patterson's side while the call was put through. Then he moved the telephone out of Patterson's reach again.

"All right, that finishes your part," he announced. "I'm going to tie you up and leave you here now."

085> Patterson looked surprised. "But I thought—"

"You thought I was going to force you to come down to the bank with me and cash that cheque?" Judd laughed. "No, Patterson, I'm not fool enough to risk a stunt like that. I planned all this six months ago, the day I saw your picture in the paper. People always said you and 090> I looked a lot alike, so I waited and grew a beard like you've done.

With a suit of your clothes on and your Panama hat I can go into that bank and collect the money without anyone knowing the difference.

I'm good at imitating voices and I know the way you hobble around. I watched you in the garden."

095> Fifteen minutes later, Judd came out of the adjoining bedroom. He wore a freshly laundered linen suit. The drooping brim of a Panama hung over his eyes.

Patterson was *lashed* to his desk chair, bound hand and foot, unable to move. Strips of adhesive plaster sealed his lips.

100> Grinning, Judd picked up the blackthorn stick which was propped against the desk. Leaning on it heavily, he practised *limping* back and forth across the room. When he felt he was proficient in this, he picked up the telephone. Imitating Patterson's deep, booming voice, he called the Penfield Taxicab Company and ordered a cab

105> to be sent out to Elm Cottage.

Then he took a pair of scissors from the desktop and hacked through the telephone wires. He tossed the instrument into the fire place.

Patterson sat with *unblinking* eyes, helpless.

When the bell rang, Judd opened the
110> front door of the cottage. The taxi driver was outside, a plump little man with a double chin and red face.

"Good afternoon, Mr. Patterson. Cab's here."

115> Judd kept his head low.

"Thank you," he said.

As he commenced to *shuffle across* the wooden porch the fat driver caught his arm and assisted him down the steps,
120> then piloted him along the garden path.

They negotiated the garden gate.

Glossary

buttonhole eyes: narrowed like an opening for a button
balked: refused to go on
deliberated: thought over carefully
sensible: showing reasonable judgment
lashed: tied
limping: walking unevenly
unblinking: showing no emotion
shuffle across: walk by dragging one's feet

"How's the old leg today, Mr. Patterson?"

Judd put extra weight on his stick. "About the same," he said gruffly. "No better."

125> The red-faced driver helped Judd into the cab, then squeezed his fat form behind the wheel. He threw a glance over his shoulder.

"Where we **bound** for today?"

"The bank."

"Okay, Mr. Patterson."

130> As the cab commenced to roll, Judd leaned back against the cushions and eased out a deep sigh of relief. In spite of himself he'd been a bit shaky. Apparently this driver knew Patterson well. The first test had been a severe one but he'd come through all right. He felt his confidence returning.

135> By the time they reached the **outskirts** of the little town of Penfield, Judd's thoughts had drifted back to the cottage. As soon as the money was safe in his hands, he'd return there, dismiss the taxi, then put a bullet through Patterson. He had intended all along to murder him. He wanted first to **gloat** over this man he hated. Hold before him

140> the wealth he had stolen. That was why he had not shot him as soon as Patterson signed the cheque.

The cab was bowling along Main Street now. In the center of the town it slid to the curb in front of the National Merchants Bank. A traffic policeman out in the center of the street was operating
145> a Stop-and-Go *stanchion*.

The driver climbed down and opened the door of the cab. As Judd alighted, he caught his arm and steered him across the sidewalk.

The door of the bank was open. On each doorpost hung a printed sign— WET PAINT!

150> Judd halted at the doorstep. He disengaged his arm from the taxi driver's.

"Thank you," he said. "I can manage now."

But the driver caught his arm again. "Better let me take you in, Mr. Patterson: I know you can make it but there's fresh paint everywhere."

"I'll be able to manage."

155> The fat driver persisted. "But you'll get your suit messed up!"

Judd was annoyed. He didn't want the man to witness the cashing of the cheque.

"Let go of me!" he snapped. "I'm not so helpless that I can't keep away from wet paint when I see a sign!" He shook his arm free and hobbled across
160> the *threshold* into the bank. The taxi driver stood staring after him.

Inside, Judd limped slowly across to the teller's cage. There were no other customers in the bank. The man behind the grille greeted him.

165>"Good afternoon, Mr. Patterson. Thanks for calling us up. Sometimes a big withdrawal like this catches us short."

Blood was pounding to Judd's face as he extracted the cheque from the pocket
170> of Patterson's suit. The teller glanced at it, stamped it, put it away in a drawer and took out a sheaf of large bills.

Glossary

bound: going; destined
outskirts: areas; outside of and near town
gloat: show great satisfaction at someone else's expense
stanchion: any post or rod used as a support
threshold: entrance

He counted the money over twice, then pushed it carelessly under the grille.

175> "There you are, Mr. Patterson. Twenty-five thousand dollars."

Judd's heart gave a little **bobble** of joy. Only with a great effort was he able to keep his hands from shaking as he picked up the money and thrust it into his wallet. Then, leaning heavily on his stick, he turned.

His jaw dropped. Every vestige of color drained from his face.

180> The fat taxi driver was entering the bank. With him was the traffic policeman from the street. The driver extended a short, thick arm, pointed at Judd excitedly.

There he is, officer—that man there. He's not Mr. Patterson!"

With an angry snarl, Judd took a step back. He dropped his stick.

185> His right hand clawed desperately for his automatic. But the officer was quicker. Before Judd could clear his weapon, an explosion **racketed** from the policeman's gun. Flying lead tore into Judd's side, spun him half around. The whole bank started to revolve, the floor tilted up and hit him.

190> When Judd opened his eyes, he was in a hospital bed. Chief Butler of the local police was standing beside him, a sarcastic smile on his lips.

"Nice of you to come back, Judd!" he said. "You had a clever **scheme.** Too bad you had to tell the taxi driver you knew enough to keep away from wet paint when you saw a sign. That was the tip-off."

195> Judd stared up from the pillow with an expression of **mingled** pain and bewilderment.

"What do you mean?" he gasped.

The police chief grinned.

"That knock over the head with the monkey 200> wrench you gave Patterson twelve years ago threw his optic nerves all out of gear. Since then he's been stone blind!

Glossary

bobble: short, jerky motion
racketed: made a loud noise
scheme: a plan
mingled: mixed

C After Reading

ACTIVITY 1

❯ Which event happened in the story?

a) Patterson saw Judd come into his house.

b) Judd put a bullet through Patterson.

c) The taxi driver found out Judd was not Patterson.

d) The police officer killed Judd in the bank.

ACTIVITY 2

❯ Reread the story to the end of line 20.

a) Why did Judd close the door noiselessly behind him?

b) What does the word "still" mean in the following sentence?

"Then he stood perfectly still, listening."			
yet	once more	nevertheless	motionless

c) When did Patterson realize there was an intruder in his house?

d) What three similarities in appearance do the men share?

❯ Now reread lines 21 to 48.

e) How does Patterson recognize Judd?

f) '"My God!" he cried in an agonized voice. "Haven't you done enough to me? Don't you know I'm—."' How do you think Patterson was going to end that sentence? Would that have changed anything in Judd's plan? Why?

g) What exactly is Patterson's job?

❯ Continue rereading from lines 49 to 134.

h) Which sentence tells the reader that Judd did not expect
Patterson to have that much money in the bank?

i) What two things did Judd do to make sure Patterson's cheque
would pass at the bank?

j) Why did Judd have to wait six months before attempting
to put his plan into action?

k) What does Judd do to make sure Patterson can't call for help?

l) What clues indicate that the taxi driver already knew
Mr. Patterson?

m) How did Judd feel when the cab started to roll toward the bank?

❯ Finally, reread from line 135 to the end of the story.

n) Why does the taxi driver insist on helping Judd (impersonating
Mr. Patterson) enter the bank?

o) Where did the taxi driver go immediately after Judd hobbled
into the bank?

p) How did Judd end up in a hospital bed?

❯ For preceding questions a, e, h and n, what do you think
Judd would be feeling at that moment? Associate each feeling
to a question letter:

surprised	determined	annoyed	powerful

ACTIVITY 3

» Go back and find clues that Mr. Patterson is blind.

Example: "His wide-open eyes did not blink." (line 22)

» Compare your answers with a partner and discuss the ones that were different. Together, compile a final list of all the clues you found and compare it with those of the rest of the class.

D Your Thoughts?

1. Why do you think Judd hates Patterson so much? What could have happened between them in the past?

2. Why do you think the story is titled "Eye-Witness"?

3. Do you think revenge can ever have a positive outcome? Explain.

4. Do you think most criminals plan their crimes in detail, like Judd? Why?

5. How do you think crimes in big cities differ from crimes in small towns?

6. What could Patterson have done to avoid the entire confrontation with Judd?

E Links to Chapter 1

» In the story, Judd experiences information overload and fails to realize that his victim is blind.

1. What emotion causes his overload? Is this typical?

2. How do our emotions affect the way we process information?

» Reread your answers in Activity 3. Explain how Judd's information overload caused him to misinterpret the clues.

F Reinvesting with Poetry

» Read this poem by William Blake and answer the questions that follow.

A POISON TREE

—By William Blake

I was angry with my friend:
I told my **wrath**, my wrath did end.
I was angry with my **foe**;
I told it not, my wrath did grow.

And I water'd it in fears,
Night & morning with my tears;
And I sunned it with my smiles
And with soft **deceitful wiles**.

And it grew both day and night,
Till it **bore** an apple bright,
And my foe **beheld** it shine,
And he knew that it was mine,

And into my garden stole
When the night had **veil'd** the **pole**:
In the morning, glad, I see
My foe **outstretch'd** beneath the tree.

> ### Glossary
> **wrath:** anger
> **foe:** enemy
> **deceitful wiles:** deviousness meant to trick; deceive
> **bore:** produced
> **beheld:** saw; observed
> **veil'd:** concealed; hid
> **pole:** a long rod
> **outstretch'd:** laid out

» Who do you think the narrator in this poem best exemplifies: Judd or Patterson? Why?

AFTER TWENTY YEARS

ABOUT THE AUTHOR

O. HENRY

O. Henry was the pen name of American William Sydney Porter. His short stories are well known for their witty narration, wordplay, warm characterization, but especially for their clever twist endings.

BORN September 11, 1862, in Greensboro, North Carolina.

QUOTE "There are stories in everything. I've got some of my best yarns from park benches, lampposts, and newspaper stands."

MORE ABOUT O. HENRY

- His type of story ending was so popular that similar endings in other stories were referred to as an O. Henry ending.
- At the age of 19, he was licensed as a pharmacist.
- When he was in his 20's, he had many different jobs such as shepherd, cook, bank teller and journalist. He started writing as a sideline.
- He died on June 5, 1910, of cirrhosis of the liver, complications of diabetes and an enlarged heart.

RECOGNITIONS INCLUDE:

- His name was given to a prestigious annual prize given to outstanding short stories.
- Several schools around the country bear Porter's pseudonym.

OTHER WORKS:

- *A Municipal Report*
- *The Gift of the Magi*
- *The Ransom of Red Chief*
- *The Cop and the Anthem*
- *A Retrieved Formation*
- *Compliments of the Season*
- *After Twenty Years*
- *Friends in San Rosario*
- *Cabbages and Kings*
- *The Four Million*

- *The Heart of the West*
- *The Gentle Grafter*
- *Options*
- *Roads of Destiny*
- *Rolling Stones*
- *Sixes and Sevens*
- *Strictly Business: More Stories of the Four Million*
- *Whirligigs*

STORY SET-UP ...

In Chapter 2, you explored the concept of being immortal by leaving your mark on other people. You also took a look at the impact of caring for others and creating a significant bond with certain people. In this story, you will read about a man who is waiting for a friend to attend an appointment made 20 years earlier. Will the other person show up? Will they recognize each other after that long? Notice how the writer gives much attention to detail and creates a clear mental picture of his story.

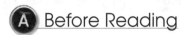

A Before Reading

ACTIVITY 1

» Select the sentence that correctly uses the bolded word from the text.

a) She'd **barely** touched the car when the alarm went off.
I went to the zoo, looking for some **barely** animals.

b) My cousin was **twirling** his mini-van down the highway.
I was **twirling** a pencil with my fingers during math class.

c) Billy was looking for Rea somewhere in this **vicinity**.
I sold all my **vicinity** to the butcher.

d) They gave it **oddly** for dinner and breakfast.
My father looked at me **oddly** when I asked him for $100.

e) I've known that young **chap** for a long time.
The tourist didn't know if he should walk or take a **chap**.

f) I was **hustling** under water, looking for fish and crabs.
You should never trust someone who spends his life **hustling**.

» With a partner, use resources to find the meanings of the following words taken from the text:

| lids (n.) | parted (v.) | hurried (v.) | fate (n.) | unfolded (v.) |

» Now write two sentences, one correct and one incorrect, for each word, as was done in a) to f). Exchange sentences with another group and complete each other's activity.

ACTIVITY 2

❯ The story you are about to read addresses the issue of friendship conflicting with personal values. For each of the following situations, explain what you would do and why:

a) Your best friend knows you never cheat, yet asks you for the answers to an exam anyway.

b) Your girlfriend/boyfriend asks you to lie to his/her parents about going to a party. You hate lying and you're not good at it.

c) Your friend since kindergarten tells you he's been stealing from a family-owned shop down your street for months and he has no intention of stopping. You know that family is not doing well financially and they're always nice to you whenever you go buy something.

B During Reading

The author effectively uses imagery to describe what is going on around the characters. Imagery involves descriptions associated with the senses.

❯ As you read the text, write down phrases that you think are especially effective at reproducing a clear image of the scene in your head. Which senses is the author eliciting with his descriptions?

AFTER TWENTY YEARS
(ADAPTED)
BY O. HENRY

The policeman **on the beat** moved up the avenue impressively. The impressiveness was habitual and not for show, since spectators were few. The time was barely 10 o'clock at night, but chilly **gust**s of wind with a taste of rain in them kept people off the streets.

005> Trying doors as he went, twirling his club with many artful movements, turning now and then to look down the calm street, the officer, with his muscular form and slight **swagger**, made a fine picture of a guardian of the peace. The vicinity was one that kept early hours. Now and then you might see the lights of a cigar store or of an all-night lunch counter;

010> but the majority of the doors belonged to business places that had long since been closed.

When about midway of a certain block the policeman suddenly slowed his walk. In the doorway of a darkened **hardware store** a man leaned, with an unlighted cigar in his mouth. As the policeman walked up to him

015> the man spoke up quickly.

"It's all right, officer," he said, reassuringly. "I'm just waiting for a friend. It's an appointment made twenty years ago. Sounds a little funny to you, doesn't it? Well, I'll explain if you'd like to make certain it's all straight. About that long ago there used to be a restaurant where this store

020> stands—'Big Joe' Brady's restaurant."

"Until five years ago," said the policeman. "It was torn down then."

The man in the doorway struck a match and lit his cigar. The light showed a pale, **square-jawed** face with sharp eyes, and a little white **scar** near his right eyebrow. His **scarfpin** was a large diamond,

025> oddly set.

"Twenty years ago tonight," said the man, "I dined here at 'Big Joe' Brady's with Jimmy Wells, my best chum, and the finest chap in the world. He and I were raised here in New York, just like two brothers, together. I was eighteen and Jimmy was twenty. The next morning

030> I was to start for the West to make my fortune. You couldn't have forced Jimmy out of New York; he thought it was the only place on earth. Well, we agreed that night that we would meet here again exactly twenty years from that date and time, no matter what our conditions might be or from what distance we might have to come. We figured
035> that in twenty years each of us should have our destiny worked out and our fortunes made, whatever they were going to be."

"It sounds pretty interesting," said the policeman. "Rather a long time between meets, though, it seems to me. Haven't you heard from your friend since you left?"

040> "Well, yes, for a time we corresponded," said the other. "But after a year or two we lost track of each other. You see, there's a lot of opportunity in the West, and I kept hustling all over the place. But I know Jimmy will meet me here if he's alive, because he always was the truest, *staunchest* old chap in the world. He'll never forget. I came a thousand
045> miles to stand in this door tonight, and it's worth it if my old partner turns up."

The waiting man pulled out a handsome watch, the lids of it set with small diamonds.

050> "Three minutes to ten," he announced. "It was exactly ten o'clock when we parted here at the restaurant door."

"Did pretty well out West, didn't you?" asked the policeman.

055> You bet! I hope Jimmy has done half as well. He was a kind of *plodder*, though, good fellow as he was. I've had to compete with some of the sharpest minds, trying to get my pay.
060> A man gets in a routine in New York. It takes the West to put a *razor-edge* on him."

Glossary

on the beat: regular route for a policeman
gusts: blasts of wind
swagger: a proud walk
hardware store: a place that sells home furnishings
square-jawed: a strong chin
scar: mark left after a injury
scarfpin: pin worn on a tie
staunchest: firm; dependable
plodder: someone who works slowly
razor-edge: as sharp as a knife

The policeman twirled his club and took a step or two.

"I'll be on my way. Hope your
065> friend comes around all right. Will you leave if he doesn't show at 10 sharp?"

"I should say not!" said the other. "I'll give him half an hour at least.
070> If Jimmy is alive on earth he'll be here by that time. So long, officer."

"Good night, sir," said the policeman, passing on along his beat, trying doors as he went.

075> There was now a fine, cold *drizzle* falling, and the wind had risen from its uncertain puffs into a steady blow. The few foot passengers walking in that quarter hurried *dismally* and silently along with coat collars turned high and pocketed hands. And in the door of the hardware store the man who had come a thousand miles to fill an appointment,
080> uncertain almost to absurdity, with the friend of his youth, smoked his cigar and waited.

About twenty minutes he waited, and then a tall man in a long overcoat, with collar turned up to his ears, hurried across from the opposite side of the street. He went directly to the waiting man.

085> "Is that you, Bob?" he asked, doubtfully.

"Is that you, Jimmy Wells?" cried the man in the door.

"Bless my heart!" exclaimed the new arrival, *grasping* both the other's hands with his own. "It's Bob, sure as *fate*. I was certain I'd find you here if you were still in existence. Well, well, well! --twenty years is a long time.
090> The old restaurant`s gone, Bob; I wish it had lasted, so we could have had another dinner there. How has the West treated you, old man?"

"*Bully*; it has given me everything I asked it for. You've changed lots, Jimmy. I never thought you were so tall by two or three inches."

"Oh, I grew a bit after I was twenty."

095> "Doing well in New York, Jimmy?"

"Moderately. I have a position in one of the city departments. Come on, Bob; we'll go around to a place I know of, and have a good long talk about old times."

The two men started up the street, arm in arm. The man from the West, 100> his egotism enlarged by success, was beginning to *outline* the history of his career. The other, submerged in his overcoat, listened with interest.

At the corner stood a drug store, brilliant with electric lights. When they came into this *glare* each of them turned simultaneously to *gaze* upon the other's face.

105> The man from the West stopped suddenly and released his arm.

"You're not Jimmy Wells," he snapped. "Twenty years is a long time, but not long enough to change a man's nose from a Roman to a pug."

"It sometimes changes a good man into a bad one," said the tall man. "You've been under arrest for ten minutes, 'Silky' Bob. Chicago thinks 110> you may have dropped over our way and informs us she wants to have a chat with you. Going quietly, are you? That's sensible. Now, before we go on to the station here's a note I was asked to hand you. You may read it here at the window. It's from Patrolman Wells."

The man from the West unfolded the little piece of paper handed him.

115> His hand was *steady* when he began to read, but it trembled a little by the time he had finished. The note was rather short.

"Bob: I was at the appointed place on 120> *time. When you struck the match to light your cigar I saw it was the face of the man wanted in Chicago. Somehow I couldn't do it myself, so I went around and got a plain clothes man to do the* 125> *job. JIMMY."*

Glossary

drizzle: light rain
dismally: gloomy; grim
grasping: gripping; holding tightly
fate: destiny
Bully: (slang) terrific
outline: summary
glare: a bright light
gaze: to look fixedly
steady: unmoving

C After Reading

ACTIVITY 1

> Understanding an unknown expression from context is an efficient and effective way of reading a text. Keep the following four points in mind when guessing the meaning from context:

- remember what the whole text is about

- reread the passage containing the word or phrase as many times as you need

- look for clues in the sentences that immediately precede or follow the word or phrase

- try to think of other contexts you've heard or seen the expression in

> With a partner, try to guess the meanings of the following expressions found in the text by applying the strategy mentioned above.

"not for show" (line 2)	"So long" (line 71)
"You bet!" (line 55)	"sure as fate" (line 88)
"it's all straight" (line 18)	"turns up" (line 46)
"torn down" (line 21)	

ACTIVITY 2

> Reread the story to the end of line 25.

a) Why were there so few people walking outside?

b) Why did Bob speak up quickly and reassuringly when the police officer approached him?

> Now reread lines 26 to 61.

c) Why did Jimmy stay in New York when Bob left?

d) What was Bob doing out West to make a living?

e) What two luxury items tell you that Bob is wealthy?

> Finally, reread from line 62 to the end of the story.

f) Why didn't Bob immediately notice that the man who ran up to him was not really Jimmy?

g) What physical trait about Jimmy did Bob find strange?

h) "I have a position in one of the city departments" (line 96). Which department is he referring to?

i) Why did Bob talk so openly about his successful career in crime?

j) How did Bob realize the other man wasn't Jimmy?

D Your Thoughts?

1. Do you think their friendship is strong enough for each of them to forgive the other? Why?

2. Why do you think Jimmy turned his friend in?

3. Did Jimmy do the right thing? Explain.

4. What would you have done if you were Jimmy?

5. How do you think Jimmy felt when he saw his friend and immediately recognized him as a criminal?

6. How far would you go to be remembered? Why?

E Links to Chapter 2

1. In Chapter 2, you learned about ways to leave your mark on other people. What proves that both Bob and Jimmy left an unforgettable impression on each other when they were younger?

2. How did Bob's and Jimmy's career choices contribute to making their mark on the world around them?

3. Who do you think had a greater impact on the world around him, Bob or Jimmy? Why?

THE BULLY

RECOGNITIONS INCLUDE:

- Many of Kiser's stories have the potential to become movies or TV shows. This story *The Bully* was adapted into a short film.

OTHER WORKS:

- *Butterflies*
- *Elvis Died at the Florida Barber College*
- *The Whale Sound*
- *The White House Boys*
- *Orphan, A True Story of Abandonment, Abuse and Redemption*
- *American Orphan*
- *Runaway, Life on the Streets*

- *For the Love of Children, Grandchildren and Pets*
- *Paying it Forward*
- *Orphanages, Reform, Schools, Jails and Prisons*
- *Dogs, Cats, Animals and Pets*
- *Stories from the Street*
- *The Joke Book*
- *The Kindness Book*
- *Pearls of Kindness*

STORY SET-UP ...

In Chapter 2, you looked at the notion of immortality: how some people try to make their mark on others around them. In this story, one of the main characters did leave a mark on the narrator; however, the way he did it is not one to take example from. The story points out that you may leave your mark on other people's lives, but it might sometimes be in a negative way. You will also be confronted with a dilemma between forgiveness and resentment.

A Before Reading

ACTIVITY 1

» Associate the following words from the story with their appropriate meaning.

WORD *Bank*

a) huddle	d) orphanage	g) limp	j) ramp
b) booth	e) burly	h) stern	
c) mumbled	f) nodded	i) Interstate	

1. Restaurant seating arrangement with a table and two benches

2. Made a quick, downward gesture of the head

3. The American equivalent of the interprovincial highway

4. Heavily built

5. Spoke in a low voice, barely articulating

6. Lacking total stiffness; soft and loose

7. A coming together of people for a purpose

8. A platform for going up and down

9. Adjective meaning with a certain hardness or severity

10. An institution that cares for children without parents

» Now write a sentence with each of the previous words. Try to link all ten sentences to make a story.

» Compare your story to someone else's. Which story components are similar and which are different?

ACTIVITY 2

❯ Read the following statements and decide where you stand on a scale of 1 (completely agree) to 5 (completely disagree). Be ready to defend your point of view with your classmates.

1. All mistakes from the distant past are forgivable.

2. Guilt can be worse than physical injury.

3. Friendship always has a price.

4. Revenge is never justified.

5. Bad people eventually get what they deserve.

ACTIVITY 3

❯ Read the title of the story and look at the illustrations. Skim quickly through the pages. Can you predict what the story is going to be about?

B During Reading

❯ As you read, take note of:

- two verbs in the negative simple past
- two verbs in the negative simple present
- two verbs in the affirmative simple past
- two verbs in the affirmative past continuous
- two verbs in the affirmative simple present

❯ At the end, compare how the author uses the past and present in the text. Why does he use the present?

THE BULLY

BY ROGER DEAN KISER

I walked into the Huddle House restaurant in Brunswick, Georgia and sat down at the counter as all of the booths were taken. I picked up a menu and began to look at the various items trying to decide if I wanted to order breakfast or just go ahead and eat lunch.

005> "Excuse me," said someone, as they touched me on the shoulder.

I looked up and turned to the side to see a rather nice looking woman standing before me.

"Is your name Roger by any chance?" she asked me.

"Yes." I responded, looking rather confused as I had never seen
010> the woman before.

"My name is Barbara and my husband is Tony," she said, pointing to a distant table near the door leading into the bathrooms.

I looked in the direction that she was pointing but I did not recognize the man who was sitting, alone at the table.

015> "I'm sorry. I'm, ah. I'm ah, confused. I don't think that I know you guys. But my name is Roger. Roger Kiser," I told her.

"Tony Claxton. Tony from Landon High School in Jacksonville, Florida?" she asked me.

"I'm really sorry. The name doesn't ***ring a bell***." I said.

020> She turned and walked back to her table and sat down. She and her husband immediately began talking and once in a while I would see her turn around in her seat and look directly at me.

I finally decided to order breakfast and a cup of decaffeinated coffee. I sat there continually ***racking my brain*** trying to remember who this
025> Tony guy was.

"I must know him," I thought to myself. "He recognizes me for some reason." I picked up my coffee and took a *sip*. All of a sudden it came to me like a flash of lightning.

"Tony. TONY THE BULL." I mumbled, as I swung myself around
030> on my stool and faced in his direction. "The bully of my seventh grade geography class," I thought.

How many times that sorry guy had made fun of my big ears in front of the girls in my class? How many times this sorry son-of-a-gun had laughed at me because I had no parents and had to live
035> in an orphanage? How many times this big bully slammed me up against the lockers in the hallway just to make himself look like a big man to all the other students?

He raised his hand and waved at me. I smiled, returned the wave and turned back around and began to eat my breakfast. "Man.
040> He's so thin now. Not the big burly guy that I remember from back in 1957," I thought to myself.

All of a sudden I heard the sound of dishes breaking so I spun around to see what had happened. Tony had accidentally hit *several* plates knocking them off the table as he was trying to get into his wheelchair
045> which had been parked in the bathroom hallway while they were eating. The waitress ran over and started picking up the broken dishes and I listened as Tony and his wife tried to *apologize*.

As Tony rolled by me, being pushed by his wife, I looked up and I smiled.

050> "Roger," he said, as he nodded his head forward.

"Tony," I responded, as I nodded my head, in return.

I watched as they went out of the door
055> and slowly made their way to a large van which had a wheelchair loader

Glossary

ring a bell: mean something
racking my brain: trying hard to remember
sip: small mouthful
several: many
apologize: offer regrets

located in the side door of the vehicle. I sat and watched as his wife tried, over and over, to get the ramp to come down. But it just would not work. Finally I got up, paid for my meal, and I walked up to the van.

060> "What's the problem?" I asked.

"Darn thing *sticks* once in a while," said Tony. "Could you help me get him in the van?" asked his wife.

"I think I can do that," I said as I grabbed the wheelchair and rolled Tony over to the passenger door.

065> I opened the door and locked the brakes on the wheelchair.

"OK. Arms around the neck, Dude," I said as I reached down and grabbed him around the waist and carefully raised him up into the passenger seat of the van.

As Tony let go of my neck I reached over and swung his limp, lifeless
070> legs, one at a time, into the van so that they would be stationed directly in front of him. "You remember. Don't you?" he said, looking directly into my eyes.

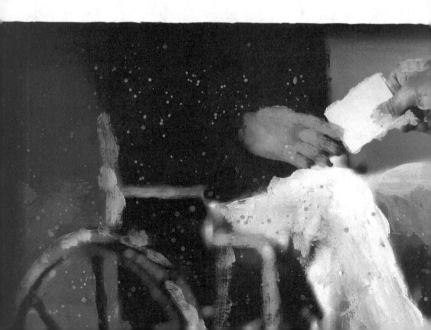

"I remember, Tony," I said.

"I guess you're thinking 'What goes around comes around,'"
075> he said, softly.

"I would never think like that, Tony," I said, with a stern look on my face.

He reached over and grabbed both of my hands and squeezed them tightly. "Is how I feel in this wheelchair how you felt way back then when you lived in the orphan home?" he asked me. "Almost, Tony.
080> You are very lucky. You have someone to push you around who loves you. I didn't have anyone." I responded.

I reached in my pocket and pulled out one of my cards that had my home telephone number written on it and I handed it to him. "Give me a call sometimes. We'll do lunch," I told him. We both laughed.

085> I stood there watching as they drove toward the interstate and finally disappeared onto the ***southbound ramp***. I hope he calls me sometime. He will be the only friend that I have from my high school days.

Glossary

sticks: does not move
southbound: moving toward the south
ramp: entrance or exit to or from a highway

C After Reading

ACTIVITY 1

» Reread the story to the end of line 25.

a) Which sentence possibly indicates the time of day?

b) Why did Roger find it strange that the woman knew his name?

c) What does Barbara tell Roger to refresh his memory about where he may know Tony from?

» Now reread lines 26 to 53.

d) Name <u>three</u> reasons why Tony picked on Roger.

e) How did Roger reply to Tony's first salutation?

f) What event embarrassed Tony inside the restaurant?

» Finally, reread from line 54 to the end of the story.

g) What gesture from Roger proves that he has forgiven Tony?

h) At line 71, Tony asks Roger if he remembers. What is he referring to?

i) What physical gesture from Tony demonstrates his sincerity and remorse towards Roger?

j) What does the last sentence tell you about Roger?

ACTIVITY 2

» Tony's comment about "What goes around comes around" (line 74) forms the central theme to this story.

a) What do you think it means?

b) Do you think this expression is true? Explain.

c) What do you believe Tony is feeling as he says those words to Roger? Why?

d) Do you believe Roger when he tells Tony that he wasn't thinking that? Why?

e) How is this expression exemplified in the text?

D Comparing the Two Stories

Notes on narrators:

A narrator is the teller of a story. Sometimes, he or she is a character in the story. Here are <u>two types of narrators</u>:

A first-person narrator tells the story using the pronouns I and me. Usually, this narrator takes part in the story, but not always. Authors use a first-person narrator to add credibility to a story, to make it look more real and personal. Sometimes you have to question this view of the events in the story, because it is a person's point of view.

A third-person narrator tells the story using the pronouns he, she, and they, but never I or me in the narration (not in dialogues). A third-person narrator is called <u>omniscient</u> when he or she can read the minds of all the characters in the story. Normally, you can trust what this narrator tells you.

1. What type of narrator is used in each story, *After Twenty Years* and *The Bully*?

2. Compare the bully in both stories using the following criteria:
   - physical appearance
   - bullying tactics used
   - motive
   - degree of premeditation

3. In both stories, the bully faces consequences for his actions. Who do you believe is worse off at the end? Why?

E Your Thoughts?

1. Which character do you pity the most? Why?

2. What do you think will happen between Tony and Roger now?

3. When a person in a couple becomes disabled, for whom is life more difficult?

4. Would you be able to forgive a bully who had made your life very difficult when you were a child? Why?

5. Which people from your past do you remember the most: people who made you feel good, or people who made you feel bad? Why?

6. '"Is how I feel in this wheelchair how you felt way back then when you lived in the orphan home?" he asked me. "Almost, Tony. You are very lucky. You have someone to push you around who loves you. I didn't have anyone."' (line 78) How do you interpret Roger's response to Tony's question?

7. Explain why you agree or disagree with the expression "time heals all wounds." Is your opinion supported or refuted by the events in the text? Why?

F Links to Chapter 2

1. What kind of people does society remember best: the famous or the infamous?

2. Can someone you've never met change your life? How?

3. Why do you believe Roger had difficulty recognizing and remembering Tony, when Tony immediately remembered Roger?

4. How can a bully affect someone's life in the long run? Could there be any positive outcome from bullying (for either the bully or the victim)?

THERE'S A MAN IN THE HABIT OF HITTING ME ON THE HEAD WITH AN UMBRELLA

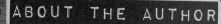

ABOUT THE AUTHOR

FERNANDO SORRENTINO

Sorrentino admits that he prefers reading to writing. Although he has been writing for over 30 years, he believes his bibliography is not all that impressive. His fans would beg to differ.

BORN November 8, 1942, in Buenos Aires, Argentina

QUOTE "A good system for revealing as yet unknown facets in man consists of placing the subject in a totally new situation and observing his reactions."

MORE ABOUT FERNANDO SORRENTINO

- His stories have been translated into English, Portuguese, Italian, German, French, Finnish, Hungarian, Polish, Chinese, Vietnamese, and Tamil.
- His writing style involves a strange combination of humour and fantasy with an added element of absurdity.
- Sorrentino has also had success in publishing several children's books.
- He often writes essays on Argentinian literature, which occasionally appear in a daily newspaper.

RECOGNITIONS INCLUDE:

- The Konex Awards merit diploma in 1994 in the category of humour.

OTHER WORKS:

- *A Lifestyle*
- *A Psychological Crusade*
- *An Enlightening Book*
- *An Enlightening Tale*
- *Chastisement by the Lambs*
- *Doctor Moreau Did It*
- *Essence and Attribute*
- *Habits of the Artichoke*
- *In Self-Defense*
- *Mere Suggestion*
- *Method for Defense Against Scorpions*
- *My Friend Luke*
- *Piccirilli*

STORY SET-UP ...

In Chapter 3, you looked at how people can become addicted to good and bad extremes and sometimes, not even realize it. In the following story, a very peculiar dependency gets imposed upon the narrator. How he deals with this extreme behaviour may decide his happiness in life.

A Before Reading

ACTIVITY 1

» Select the best word for each blank:

WORD Bank

bludgeon (v.)	uproarious (adj.)	interminable (adj.)
impervious (adj.)	animosity (n.)	foreboding (n.)
sultry (adj.)		

1. I know she hates me. I can sense the …

2. My raincoat is completely … to rain.

3. Tropical countries often have humid, … days.

4. Cavemen would spear or … their prey.

5. Everyone had an … time at the party.

6. I feel a certain … about tomorrow's exam.

7. The wait at the doctor's office was …

ACTIVITY 2

» In the story, the narrator is forced to deal with a very strange man who has a very strange habit.

a) Rank the following absurd habits from 1 (least absurd) to 5 (most absurd) and discuss your choices with a partner.

  - Your downstairs neighbour only walks backwards.

  - Greg will never use a bathroom other than his own.

  - Caroline sings everything she says.

  - Peter brings his lucky skunk everywhere he goes.

  - Anna always greets her friends with a slap in the face.

b) How would you convince each of the people in the previous scenarios to put an end to their habit?

ACTIVITY 3

» How do you deal with annoying people? Give concrete examples of experiences you have actually had.

» What are the most annoying habits people have in public?

» Do you have any habits that annoy others? How do you know this?

B During Reading

» The author uses several adverbs to describe the way the man hits the narrator with his umbrella. As you read, note these adverbs, and then choose the portrait you think they create about the man.

Is the man ...		
mean?	intimidating?	lazy?
arrogant?	committed?	likeable?

» Explain your choice.

*Remember: adverbs modify verbs, adjectives or other adverbs. They usually end in -*ly*.
Ex.: He *gently* placed the vase back on the table.

THERE'S A MAN IN THE HABIT OF HITTING ME ON THE HEAD WITH AN UMBRELLA

BY FERNANDO SORRENTINO

(Translation: Clark M. Zlotchew)

There's a man in the habit of hitting me on the head with an umbrella. It makes exactly five years today that he's been hitting me on the head with his umbrella. At first I couldn't stand it; now I'm used to it.

005> I don't know his name. I know he's average in appearance, wears a gray suit, is graying at the temples, and has a common face. I met him five years ago one sultry morning. I was sitting on a tree-shaded bench in Palermo Park, reading the paper. Suddenly I felt something touch my head. It was the very same man who now, as I'm writing, keeps *whacking* me, mechanically and impassively, with an umbrella.

010> On that occasion I turned around filled with *indignation:* he just kept on hitting me. I asked him if he was crazy: he didn't even seem to hear me. Then I threatened to call a policeman. Unperturbed, *cool as a cucumber*, he stuck with his task. After a few moments of indecision, and seeing that he was not about to change his attitude, I stood up and

015> punched him in the nose. The man fell down, and let out an almost inaudible moan. He immediately got back on his feet, apparently with great effort, and without a word again began hitting me on the head with the umbrella. His nose was bleeding and, at that moment, I felt sorry for him. I felt remorse for having hit him so hard. After all, the

020> man wasn't exactly bludgeoning me; he was merely tapping me lightly with his umbrella, not causing any pain at all. Of course, those taps were extremely *bothersome*. As we all know, when a fly lands on your

forehead, you don't feel any pain whatsoever; what you feel is ***annoyance***.
Well then, that umbrella was one ***humongous*** fly that kept landing
025> on my head time after time, and at regular intervals.

Convinced that I was dealing with a madman, I tried to escape. But the
man followed me, wordlessly continuing to hit me. So I began to run
(at this juncture I should point out that not many people run as fast
as I do). He took off after me, vainly trying to land a blow. The man
030> was huffing and puffing and gasping so, that I thought if I continued
to force him to run at that speed, my ***tormentor*** would drop dead
right then and there.

That's why I slowed down to a walk. I looked at him. There was no trace
of either gratitude or reproach on his face. He merely kept hitting me
035> on the head with the umbrella. I thought of showing up at the police
station and saying, "Officer, this man is hitting me on the head with
an umbrella." It would have been an unprecedented case. The officer
would have looked at me suspiciously, would have asked for my papers,
and begun asking embarrassing questions. And he might even have
040> ended up placing me under arrest.

I thought it best to return home. I took the 67 bus. He, all the while
hitting me with his umbrella, got on
behind me. I took the first seat. He
stood right beside me, and held on
045> to the railing with his left hand. With
his right hand he ***unrelentingly*** kept
whacking me with that umbrella. At first,
the passengers exchanged timid smiles.
The driver began to observe us in
050> the rearview mirror. Little by little
the bus trip turned into one great fit
of laughter, an uproarious, interminable
fit of laughter. I was burning with
shame. My persecutor, impervious to
055> the laughter, continued to strike me.

Glossary

whacking: hitting hard
indignation: anger
cool as a cucumber: calm
bothersome: causing
irritation
annoyance: impatience;
irritation
humongous: very large
tormentor: someone who
causes suffering
unrelentingly: without
stopping

I got off—we got off—at Pacífico Bridge. We walked along Santa Fe Avenue. Everyone stupidly turned to stare at us. It occurred to me to say to them, "What are you looking at, you idiots? Haven't you ever seen a man hit another man on the head with an umbrella?"
060> But it also occurred to me that they probably never had seen such a spectacle. Then five or six little boys began chasing after us, shouting like maniacs.

But I had a plan. Once I reached my house, I tried to slam the door in his face. That didn't happen. He must have read my mind, because
065> he firmly seized the doorknob and pushed his way in with me.

From that time on, he has continued to hit me on the head with his umbrella. As far as I can tell, he has never either slept or eaten anything. His sole activity consists of hitting me. He is with me in everything I do, even in my most intimate activities. I remember
070> that at first, the blows kept me awake all night. Now I think it would be impossible for me to sleep without them.

Still and all, our relations have not always been good. I've asked him, on many occasions, and in all possible tones, to explain his behavior to me. **To no avail**: he has wordlessly continued to hit me on the head
075> with his umbrella. Many times I have let him have it with punches,

kicks, and even—God forgive me—umbrella blows. He would ***meekly***
accept the blows. He would accept them as though they were part
of his job. And this is precisely the weirdest aspect of his personality:
that unshakable faith in his work coupled with a complete lack of
080> animosity. In short, that conviction that he was carrying out some
secret mission that responded to a higher authority.

Despite his lack of physiological needs, I know that when I hit him,
he feels pain. I know he is weak. I know he is mortal.

I also know that I could be rid of him with a single bullet. What
085> I don't know is if it would be better for that bullet to kill him or to kill
me. Neither do I know if, when the two of us are dead, he might not
continue to hit me on the head with his umbrella. In any event, this
reasoning is pointless; I recognize that I would never dare to kill him
or kill myself.

090> On the other hand, I have recently come to the realization that I couldn't
live without those blows. Now, more and more frequently, a certain
foreboding overcomes me. A new anxiety is eating at my soul: the
anxiety stemming from the thought that this man, perhaps when I need
him most, will depart and I will no longer feel those umbrella taps that
095> helped me sleep so ***soundly***.

Glossary

to no avail: of no use
meekly: quietly
soundly: deeply

C After Reading

ACTIVITY 1

❯❯ Reread the story to the end of line 25.

a) What clue in the introduction tells the reader that the story is about a habit the narrator can't break?

b) Why does the narrator feel pity for the man with the umbrella?

❯❯ Now reread lines 26 to 40.

c) Why does the narrator slow down when he tries to run away from the man with the umbrella?

d) Why would the police arrest the narrator if he went to a police station?

❯❯ Finally, reread from line 41 to the end of the story.

e) Why doesn't the narrator just kill his tormentor?

f) What concerns the narrator the most about the man with the umbrella?

ACTIVITY 2

❯❯ Give the story a new conclusion by guessing what would happen if:

- The narrator actually went to the police station.

- The man with the umbrella left just as unexpectedly as he arrived.

- The man with the umbrella started speaking.

- The narrator killed his tormentor.

Your Thoughts?

1. What would you do if you were the narrator?

2. Which part(s) of the story do you consider unbelievable? Why?

3. Do you think the narrator tried hard enough to get rid of the man with the umbrella? Why?

E Links to Chapter 3

❖ Associate each of the following features (a to e), common to many addictions, to a sentence from the story (1 to 5) that best represents it.

a) Initial experience with habit is not always pleasant.

b) Addict tries to quit or resist habit on his own.

c) Addict tries to justify habit to himself.

d) Addict seeks help from someone else.

e) Addict cannot imagine life without his habit.

1) I thought of showing up at the police station ... (line 35)

2) On that occasion I turned around ... (line 10)

3) Now I think it would be impossible for me to sleep without them. (line 70)

4) Many times I have let him have it ... (line 75)

5) After all, the man wasn't exactly bludgeoning ... (line 20)

F Reinvesting with Poetry

» Read this anonymous poem and answer the questions that follow.

I AM HABIT

—By Anonymous

I am your constant companion.

I am your greatest asset or heaviest burden.

I will push you up to success or down to disappointment.

I am at your command.

Half the things you do might just as well be turned over to me,

For I can do them quickly, correctly, and profitably.

I am easily managed, just be firm with me.

Those who are great, I have made great.

Those who are failures, I have made failures.

I am not a machine, though I work with the precision

of a machine and the intelligence of a person.

You can run me for profit, or you can run me for ruin.

Show me how you want it done. Educate me. Train me.

Lead me. Reward me.

And I will then … do it automatically.

I am your servant.

Who am I?

I am habit.

» Which lines in the poem would the man with the umbrella most likely tell his victim? Why?

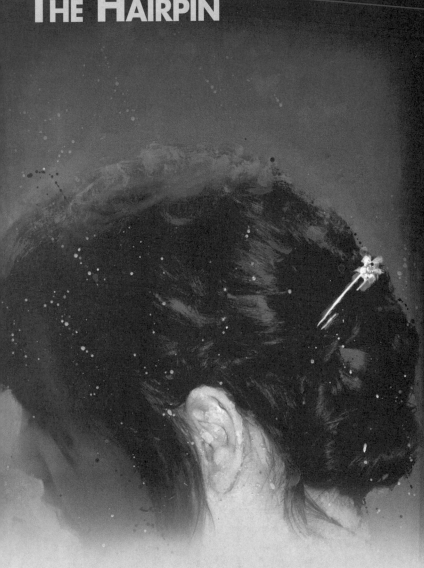

THE HAIRPIN

ABOUT THE AUTHOR

GUY DE MAUPASSANT

It seemed like Guy de Maupassant was destined from youth to excel in the literary arts. When he was young, his mother enjoyed classic literature and read lots of Shakespeare. After graduation, De Maupassant was mentored by the great author Gustave Flaubert.

BORN August 5, 1850, near Dieppe, France

QUOTE "It is the lives we meet that make life worth living."

MORE ABOUT GUY DE MAUPASSANT

- At 20 years old, he volunteered for military service during the Franco-Prussian conflict.
- In the 1880s, he composed over 300 works of literature, most of which were short stories.
- Critics consider *Boule de Suif* to be his greatest masterpiece.
- He enjoyed being alone and meditating for long periods of time, yet he also enjoyed travelling and meeting people.
- In 1892, he attempted suicide and was committed to an asylum in Paris.

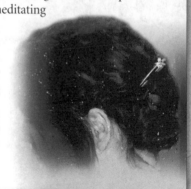

RECOGNITIONS INCLUDE:

- He is the subject of Tolstoy's *The Works of Guy de Maupassant*.
- Friedrich Nietzsche refers to him in his autobiography.

OTHER WORKS:

- *The Terror*
- *The Adopted Son*
- *The Baroness*
- *The Beggar*
- *A Coup d'Etat*
- *A Duel*
- *Farewell*
- *The Diamond Necklace*
- *Forgiveness*
- *The Horrible*
- *In the Spring*
- *Julie Romaine*
- *A Woman's Life*
- *Madame Baptiste*
- *Martine*
- *A Meeting*

STORY SET-UP · · ·

In Chapter 3, you learned that a desire for something or a passion for someone can be taken to the extreme. In this story, you will see that certain types of relationships create dependencies that may be perceived as addiction: someone gets "hooked" on someone else. In the following story, you'll read about how one man's obsession with a woman drove him to an extreme lifestyle.

A Before Reading

ACTIVITY 1

» Select the correct meaning for the bolded words.

1. It was hot—a relaxing heat, scented of the rich **soil**.
   a) people   b) earth   c) flowers

2. […] he had in this way **amassed** a fortune by his constant labour.
   a) accumulated   b) missed   c) found

3. Up at **dawn**, going over his fields until night, always on the watch […]
   a) early morning   b) midday   c) early evening

4. […] tortured by an uncontrollable desire for money, which nothing can **appease**.
   a) steal   b) seize   c) calm

5. There, look at this little white **speck** on my left eye.
   a) insect   b) dot   c) pin

6. And if I did but tell you what an **agonizing** life I had led with her!
   a) fun-filled   b) boring   c) painful

7. I felt a mad **impulse** to open my arms, to take her to me and strangle her.
   a) desire   b) heartbeat   c) comedy

ACTIVITY 2

❯ Discuss with a partner what you believe the following passages from the text indicate about the kind of relationship the couple had:

- *He murmured: "I love her," as if he had said: "I am dying."*

- *"Ah, for three years, what a distracting and glorious life we lived!"*

- *"Five or six times I all but killed her; she tried to pierce my eyes with that pin at which you have been looking."*

- *"We loved each other! How can I explain such a passion?"*

- *"When I looked at her, I wanted to kill her as sharply as I wanted to embrace her."*

B During Reading

The setting of a story is usually the environment described by the author in which characters exist and interact. Certain elements described in a setting may include:

- the climate/time of day/year
- pertinent locations and places
- important objects
- character traits (physical or personality)

❯ As you read the story, take notes on its setting based on the preceding elements and any other you believe are significant.

THE HAIRPIN
(ADAPTED)

BY GUY DE MAUPASSANT

remember neither the country nor the name of the man concerned. It was far, very far from this part of the world, on a fertile and *scorching* sea-coast. All morning we had been following a coast clothed with crops and a blue sea clothed in sunlight. It was hot—a relaxing heat,
005> scented of the rich soil.

I had been told that, in the evening, I could obtain hospitality in the house of a Frenchman, who lived at the end of a cliff, in an orange *grove*. Who was he? I did not yet know. He had arrived one morning, ten years ago; he had bought a piece of ground, planted vines and
010> seed; he had worked, this man, passionately, furiously. Then, month by month, year by year, increasing his land, continually fertilising the virgin soil, he had in this way amassed a fortune by his constant labour.

Yet he went on working, all the time, people said. Up at dawn, going over his fields until night, always on the watch, he seemed to be *goaded*
015> by a fixed idea, tortured by an uncontrollable desire for money, which nothing can appease. Now he seemed to be very rich.

The sun was just setting when I reached his *dwelling*. This was, indeed, built at the end of an out-thrust cliff, in the middle of orange-trees. It was a large plain-looking house, built four-square, and overlooking the sea.
020> As I approached, a man with a big beard appeared in the door way. Greeting him, I asked him to give me *shelter* for the night. He held out his hand to me, smiling. "Come in, sir, and make yourself at home."

He led the way to a room, put a servant at my disposal, with the perfect assurance and easy good manners of a man of the world; then he left me,
025> saying: "We will dine as soon as you are quite ready to come down."

We did indeed dine alone, on a terrace facing the sea. At the beginning of the meal, I spoke to him of this country, so rich, so far from the world, so little known. He smiled, answering indifferently.

"Yes, it is a beautiful country. But no country is attractive that lies
030> so far from the country of one's heart."

"You regret France?"

"I regret Paris."

"Why not go back to it?"

"Oh, I shall go back to it."

035> Then, quite naturally, we began to talk of French society, of the boulevards,
and people, and things of Paris. He questioned me like a man who knew
all about it, mentioning names, all the names familiar on the Vaudeville
promenade.

"Who goes to Tortoni's now?"

040>"All the same people, except those who have died."

I looked at him closely, haunted by a vague memory. Assuredly I had
seen this face somewhere. But where? But when?

"Do you know Boutrelle?"

"Yes, well."

045>"Is he much changed?"

"Yes, he has aged."

"And La Ridamie?"

"Always the same."

"And the women? Tell me about the women. Let me see, Do you know
050> Suzanne Verner?"

"Yes, very **stout**. Done for."

"Ah! And Sophie Astier?"

"Dead."

"Poor girl! And is … do you know … "

055> But he was abruptly silent. Then
in a changed voice, his face grown
suddenly pale, he went on:

Glossary

scorching: burning hot
grove: small group of trees
goaded: driven
dwelling: house
shelter: a safe place to stay
stout: large; heavy

"No, it would be better for me not to speak of it any more, it tortures me."

060> Then, as if to change his thoughts, he rose.

"Shall we go in?"

"I am quite ready."

And he preceded me into the house.

065> My host smiled.

"It is the dwelling, or rather the **hovel**, of an exile," said he, "but my room is rather more decent. Let's go there."

My first thought, when I entered the room, was that I was entering
070> into a second-hand dealer's, so full of things was it. On the walls two excellent pictures by well-known artists, hangings, weapons, swords and pistols, and then, right in the middle of the most **prominent** panel, a square of white satin in a gold frame.

Surprised, I went closer to look at it and I saw a hairpin stuck
075> in the centre of the shining material.

My host laid his hand on my shoulder.

"There," he said, with a smile, "is the only thing I ever look at in this place, and the only one I have seen for ten years, I can say: 'This pin is the whole of my life!'"

080> I ended by saying: "Some woman has made you suffer?"

He went on **harshly**: "I suffer yet, and frightfully … But come on to my balcony. A name came to my lips just now, that I dared not say, because if you had answered 'dead,' as you did for Sophie Astier, I should have lost my mind, this very day."

085> He continued: "Is Jeanne de Limours still alive?"

His eye was fixed on mine, full of **shuddering** terror. I smiled.

"Very much alive … and prettier than ever."

"You know her?"

"Yes."

090> He hesitated: "Intimately?"

"No."

He took my hand:

"Talk to me about her."

"But there is nothing I can
095> say: she is one of the women,
or rather one of the most
charming and expensive
social ladies in Paris. She leads
a pleasant and ***sumptuous*** life, and that's all one can say."

100> He murmured: "I love her," as if he had said: "I am dying." Then
abruptly: "Ah, for three years, what a distracting and glorious life we
lived! Five or six times I all but killed her; she tried to pierce my eyes
with that pin at which you have been looking. There, look at this little
white speck on my left eye. We loved each other! How can I explain
105> such a passion? You would not understand it.

"There must be a gentle love, born of the mutual union of two hearts
and two souls; but surely there exists a savage love, cruelly tormenting
two conflicting beings who adore while they hate.

"That girl ruined me in three years. I had four million which she devoured
110> with a sweet smile that seemed to die from her eyes on to her lips.

"You know her? There is something
irresistible about her. What is it?
I don't know. For three years I was
conscious of no one but her. How
115> I suffered! For she deceived me with
everyone. Why? For no reason, for
the mere sake of deceiving. And when
I discovered it, she admitted it calmly.
'We're not married, are we?' she said."

Glossary

hovel: a shack
prominent: something
that stands out
harshly: use an
unpleasant tone
shuddering: shaking
sumptuous: luxurious; rich

120> He was silent. Then, some minutes later:

"When I had **squandered** my last sou for her, she said to me quite simply: 'You realise, my dear, that I cannot live on air and sunshine. I love you madly, I love you more than anyone in the world, but one must live. Poverty and I would never make good partners.'

125>"And if I did but tell you what an agonizing life I had led with her! When I looked at her, I wanted to kill her as sharply as I wanted to embrace her. When I looked at her … I felt a mad impulse to open my arms, to take her to me and strangle her. There **lurked** in her, behind her eyes, something treacherous and forever **unattainable** that made
130> me detest her; and it is perhaps because of that that I loved her so.

And look you, when I went out with her, she fixed her glance on every man, in such a way that she seemed to be giving each one of them her complete interest. That maddened me and yet held me to her the closer. Do you understand?

135>"And what torture! At the theatre, in the restaurant, it seemed to me that men possessed her under my very eyes. And as soon as I left her company, other men did indeed possess her.

"It is ten years since I have seen her, and I love her more than ever."

Night had spread its wings upon the earth. The powerful scent of
140> orange-trees hung in the air.

I said to him: "You will see her again?"

He answered: "By God, yes. I have here, in land and money, from seven to eight hundred thousand francs. When the million is complete, I shall sell all and depart. I shall have enough for one year with her—one entire
145> marvellous year. And then goodbye, my life will be over."

I asked:"But afterwards?"

"Afterwards, I don't know. It will be the end. Perhaps I shall ask her to keep me
150> on as her servant."

Glossary

squandered: wasted
lurked: laid hidden especially for evil purposes
unattainable: unable to be reached

C After Reading

ACTIVITY 1

>> Read the quotes from the story and answer the questions that follow:

"Up at dawn, going over his fields until night, always on the watch, he seemed to be goaded by a fixed idea, tortured by an uncontrollable desire for money, which nothing can appease."

a) Who says this line?

b) What does this say about the man's degree of obsession?

c) Why was he so obsessed with making money?

"There is the only thing I ever look at in this place, and the only one I have seen for ten years, I can say: 'This pin is the whole of my life!'"

a) Who says this line?

b) How do you know the pin is important to him?

c) Why is that pin so important to him?

ACTIVITY 2

>> Reread the story to the end of line 25.

a) Where was the Frenchman's house located?

b) How did he accumulate his riches?

c) Why does the narrator visit the Frenchman?

>> Now reread from lines 26 to 64.

d) What do the narrator and the Frenchman have in common?

e) Why does the Frenchman hesitate to ask about someone and then abruptly go silent?

�»› Continue rereading from lines 65 to 99.

f) What passage from the text indicates that the Frenchman has many valuable possessions?

g) How does the narrator describe the woman the Frenchman is obsessed with?

�»› Finally, reread from line 100 to the end of the story.

h) Why did Jeanne de Limours leave the Frenchman?

i) Why did he love her so much?

j) How will he try to stay with her after his money runs out again?

D Comparing the Two Stories

�»› In both "There's a Man in the Habit of Hitting Me on the Head with an Umbrella" and "The Hairpin," the main character suffers because of his obsession. With a partner, discuss:

– How each man suffered and who you believe suffered more.

– How each man tried to deal with his tormentor.

– Whether each was victorious in defeating his "addiction."

E Your Thoughts?

1. Who do you respect less: the Frenchman or Jeanne? Why?

2. Was he in love or infatuated? What's the difference?

3. Do you believe Jeanne was ever really in love with him? Why?

F Links to Chapter 3

1. The Frenchman took his interest to the extreme. Give examples of things he did that only someone who is "hooked" would do.

2. What is Jeanne de Limours hooked on?

EXAMINATION DAY

HENRY SLESAR

Slesar was a very prolific and accomplished author, but many remember him mostly for the work he did for TV shows such as *Alfred Hitchcock Presents* and *Batman*. The story you are about to read was adapted for TV in an episode of *The Twilight Zone*.

BORN June 12, 1927, in Brooklyn, N.Y.

QUOTE (to an actress on a soap opera he once wrote for): "I love making you suffer, because you suffer so well."

MORE ABOUT HENRY SLESAR

- He wrote over 500 short stories throughout his career.
- He also wrote under the pseudonyms O.H. Leslie, E.K. Jarvis and Jay Street.
- He originated the phrase "coffee break."
- He started his career in publishing as a copywriter at the age of 17.
- He was a science fiction writer in the first decade of his career, but by 1980, he was better known as a mystery writer.
- His TV writing career also took him to Europe, where he continued to write soap operas.
- He died in April of 2002, of natural causes at the age of 74.

RECOGNITIONS INCLUDE:

- In 1974, he received an Emmy for the TV series *The Edge of Night*.
- He was recipient of the Mystery Writers of America Edgar Award, which he won twice in his career.
- TV Guide once called him the "Writer with the Biggest Audience in America."

OTHER WORKS:

- *Murder at Heartbreak Hospital*
- *Thing at the Door*
- *Dream Town*
- *The Delegate from Venus*
- *My Father, the Cat*
- *Reluctant Genius*
- *The Success Machine*
- *20 Million Miles to Earth*
- *I, Monster*
- *The Gray Flannel Shroud*
- *Acrostic Mysteries*
- *Inspector Cross*
- *The Jam*
- *Survivor 1*
- *After*
- *Chief*
- *Doctor*
- *Merchant*
- *Bats*

STORY SET-UP ...

In Chapter 4, you learned how control and manipulation are done, more often than not, in a subtle and sneaky way. People often have to resort to mind games to get others to do what they want. In *Examination Day*, you will read about how control is imposed in a fictional society where intelligence is everything.

A Before Reading

ACTIVITY 1

» Select the sentence containing the correctly used bolded word from the text.

a) They bought some **moistness** at the bookstore.
The **moistness** of the morning grass wet my feet.

b) I left the milk out and it **spoiled**.
Tom **spoiled** his way to school.

c) The receptionist **greeted** me when I arrived.
Tanya **greeted** the horse a nutritious meal.

d) They **peered** down the street at a very fast speed.
He **peered** through the window to see if it was raining.

e) I was looking for some **abruptness** in the box.
My car stopped with a violent **abruptness**.

f) I **hesitantly** gave the big dog a bone.
Tamara hurried to the store **hesitantly**.

g) The **puzzlement** was cheaper next door.
I looked at my teacher with **puzzlement**.

h) The cat **concealed** with the baby kittens.
Amanda was **concealed** from the sun.

ACTIVITY 2

» The following questions are based on issues mentioned
in the text. With a partner, discuss:

a) How the government uses laws and penalties to control its
citizens. How does this apply to teenagers in particular?

b) How the words "Examination Day" make you feel. Why?

c) The worst thing that can happen to someone who fails a test.
The best thing that can happen to someone who passes a test.

d) How parents affect a teenager's academic performance
at school.

B During Reading

» Look at the descriptive language the author uses. Write down
some phrases that you think are particularly effective:

Example:

Descriptive language	... and the anxious manner of her speech caused her husband to answer sharply.

EXAMINATION DAY

BY HENRY SLESAR

The Jordans never spoke of the exam, not until their son, Dickie, was twelve years old. It was on his birthday that Mrs Jordan first mentioned the subject in his presence, and the anxious manner of her speech caused her husband to answer sharply.

005> 'Forget about it,' he said. 'He'll do all right.'

They were at breakfast table, and the boy looked up from his plate curiously. He was an alert-eyed youngster with flat blond hair and a quick, nervous manner. He didn't understand what the sudden tension was about, but he did know that today was his birthday,
010> and he wanted harmony above all. Somewhere in the little apartment there were wrapped, **beribboned** packages waiting to be opened, and in the tiny wall-kitchen something warm and sweet was being prepared in the automatic stove. He wanted the day to be happy, and the moistness of his mother's eyes, the **scowl** on his father's face,
015> spoiled the mood of **fluttering** expectation with which he had greeted the morning.

'What exam?' he asked.

His mother looked at the tablecloth. 'It's just a sort of Government Intelligence test they give children at the age of twelve. You'll be taking
020> it next week. It's nothing to worry about.'

'You mean a test like in school?'

'Something like that,' his father said, getting up from the table. 'Go and read your comics, Dickie.' The boy rose and **wandered** towards that part of the living room which had been 'his' corner since infancy. He fingered
025> the topmost comic of the stack, but seemed uninterested in the colourful squares of fast-paced action. He wandered towards the window, and peered **gloomily** at the veil of mist that **shrouded** the glass.

'Why did it have to rain today?' he said. 'Why couldn't it rain tomorrow?'

His father, now **slumped** into an armchair with the Government
030> newspaper rattled the sheets in **vexation**. 'Because it just did, that's all. Rain makes the grass grow.'

'Why, Dad?'

'Because it does, that's all.'

Dickie **puckered** his brow. 'What makes it green, though?
035> The grass?'

'Nobody knows,' his father snapped, then immediately regretted his abruptness.

Later in the day, it was birthday time again. His mother beamed as she handed over the gaily-coloured packages, and even his father
040> managed a grin and a **rumple**-of-the-hair. He kissed his mother and shook hands gravely with his father. Then the birthday cake was brought forth, and the ceremonies concluded.

An hour later, seated by the window,
he watched the sun force its way
045> between the clouds.

'Dad,' he said, 'how far away is the sun?'

'Five thousand miles,' his father said.

***

Dickie sat at the breakfast table and
again saw moisture in his mother's eyes.
050> He didn't connect her tears with the
exam until his father suddenly brought
the subject to light again.

Glossary

beribboned: wrapped in ribbons
scowl: frown
fluttering: nervous; exciting;
wandered: walked without a fixed goal
gloomily: in a depressed mood
shrouded: covered
slumped: sat in a drooping posture
vexation: annoyed manner
puckered: wrinkled
rumple: to mess

'Well, Dickie,' he said, with a manly **frown**, 'you've got an appointment today.'

055> 'I know Dad. I hope –'

'Now, it's nothing to worry about. Thousands of children take this test every day. The Government wants to know how smart you are, Dickie. That's all there is to it.'

'I get good marks in school,' he said hesitantly.

060> 'This is different. This is a—special kind of test. They give you this stuff to drink, you see, and then you go into a room where there's a sort of machine—'

'What stuff to drink?' Dickie said.

'It's nothing. It tastes like peppermint. It's just to make sure you answer
065> the questions truthfully. Not that the Government thinks you won't tell the truth, but it makes sure.'

Dickie's face showed puzzlement, and a touch of fright. He looked at his mother, and she composed her face into a **misty** smile.

'Everything will be all right,' she said.

070> 'Of course it will,' his father agreed. 'You're a good boy, Dickie; you'll make out fine. Then we'll come home and celebrate. All right?'

'Yes sir,' Dickie said.

They entered the Government Educational Building fifteen minutes before the appointed hour. They crossed the marble floors of the great

075> **pillared** lobby, passed beneath an archway and entered an automatic lift that brought them to the fourth floor.

There was a young man wearing an insignia-less **tunic**, seated at a polished desk in front of Room 404. He held a clipboard in his hand, and he checked the list down to the Js and permitted the

080> Jordans to enter.

The room was as cold and official as a courtroom, with long benches **flanking** metal tables. There were several fathers and sons already there, and a thin-lipped woman with **cropped** black hair was passing out sheets of paper.

085> Mr Jordan filled out the form, and returned it to the clerk. Then he told Dickie: 'It won't be long now. When they call your name, you just go through the doorway at the end of the room.' He indicated the portal with his finger.

Glossary

frown: a facial expression of displeasure or concern
misty: tearful
pillared: with columns
tunic: a loose-fitting piece of clothing
flanking: placed beside
cropped: cut short

A concealed loudspeaker *crackled* and called off the first name. Dickie
090> saw a boy leave his father's side *reluctantly* and walk slowly towards
the door.

At five minutes to eleven, they called the name of Jordan.

'Good luck, son,' his father said, without looking at him. 'I'll call
for you when the test is over.'

095> Dickie walked to the door and turned the knob. The room inside was
dim, and he could barely make out the features of the grey-tunicked
attendant who greeted him.

'Sit down,' the man said softly. He indicated a high stool beside his desk.
'Your name's Richard Jordan?'

100> 'Yes, sir.'

'Your classification number is 600-115. Drink this, Richard.'

He lifted a plastic cup from the desk and handed it to the boy. The
liquid inside had the consistency of buttermilk, tasted only vaguely
of the promised peppermint. Dickie downed it, and handed the man
105> the empty cup.

He sat in silence, feeling *drowsy*, while the man wrote busily on a sheet
of paper. Then the attendant looked at his watch, and rose to stand
only inches from Dickie's face. He unclipped a penlike object from
the pocket of his tunic, and flashed a tiny light into the boy's eyes.

110> 'All right,' he said. 'Come with me, Richard.'

He led Dickie to the end of the room, where a single wooden armchair
faced a multi-dialled computing machine. There was a microphone
on the left arm of the chair, and when the boy sat down, he found
its pinpoint head conveniently at his mouth.

115> 'Now just relax, Richard. You'll be asked some questions, and you
think them over carefully. Then give your answers into the microphone.
The machine will take care of the rest.'

'Yes, sir.'

'I'll leave you alone now. Whenever you want to start, just say "ready"
120> into the microphone.'

'Yes, sir.'

The man squeezed his shoulder, and left.

Dickie said, 'Ready.'

Lights appeared on the machine, and a mechanism *whirred*. A voice
125> said: 'Complete this sequence. One, four, seven, ten …'

Mr and Mrs Jordan were in the living room, not speaking, not even
speculating.

It was almost four o'clock when the telephone rang. The woman tried
to reach it first, but her husband was quicker.

130> 'Mr Jordan?'

The voice was clipped: a *brisk*, official voice.

'Yes, speaking.'

'This is the Government Educational Service. Your son, Richard
M Jordan, Classification 600-115 has completed the Government
135> examination. We regret to inform you that his intelligence quotient
is above the Government regulation, according to Rule 84 Section 5
of the New Code.'

Across the room, the woman cried out,
knowing nothing except the emotion
140> she read on her husband's face.

'You may specify by telephone,' the voice
droned on, 'whether you wish his body
interred by the Government, or would
you prefer a private burial place? The
145> fee for Government burial is ten dollars.'

Glossary

crackled: made snapping noises
reluctantly: not eager
drowsy: sleepy
whirred: made a soft swishing sound
brisk: quick and efficient
droned on: talk in a flat voice

C After Reading

ACTIVITY 1

❯❯ The shocking ending is preceded by many examples of tension and anxiety throughout the story.

a) Find three adjectives or adverbs that reflect this tone.

b) What is so particularly shocking about the very last sentence?

ACTIVITY 2

❯❯ Reread the story to the end of line 27.

a) How do Dickie's parents feel on his birthday?

b) What two things is Dickie looking forward to?

❯❯ Now reread from lines 28 to 47.

c) How do we know that Dickie is a curious young man?

d) Why does his father refuse to properly answer Dickie's simple questions?

❯❯ Continue rereading from lines 48 to 69.

e) Why did his mother's eyes begin to water?

f) Why will Dickie have to drink a certain liquid before the test?

g) Which sentence first tells the reader that Dickie may be sensing fear?

❯❯ Next reread from line 70 to 125.

h) What does the author compare the waiting room to?

i) What does the father tell Dickie to comfort him?

j) What clue in Dickie's behaviour indicates to the reader that he doesn't know what the test is really about?

k) Why do you think a computer administers the test and not a person?

> Finally, reread from line 126 to the end of the story.

l) How do you know that the air is very tense between the parents as they await the test results?

m) What is the first word the father hears on the phone that tells him he is going to get bad news?

n) Why does Dickie "fail" the test?

D Your Thoughts?

1. Why do you think "The Jordans never spoke of the exam, not until their son, Dickie, was twelve years old." (line 2)?

2. What possible reasons can the government have for eliminating children with high IQs?

3. Would you be able to work at the government building described in the story? Why?

4. What do you think 12-year-old Dickie would have done if he had known the truth behind the test?

E Links to Chapter 4

1. How does keeping a population's IQ low guarantee easy control for the government?

2. What are the risks and dangers involved in having so much control over so many people?

3. What is more important to you: equality and conformity for all or uniqueness and free choice?

4. Do you believe intelligence and charm are connected? Why?

F Reinvesting with Poetry

» Read this anonymous poem and answer the questions
that follow.

BOW YOUR HEAD

—By Anonymous

I wish I knew what I did wrong,
Why do you go and treat me this way?
All I do is study day and night long,
While you mock and point and laugh away.

It's true, I'm smart and only have one friend,
And you, well, you've got lots and lots.
But we'll see what happens at the end;
When the time comes, *you* will call *me* 'boss'.

» How are intelligent people persecuted in the following?

- *Examination Day*
- this poem
- society

» Who do you think the title applies to the most: the narrator
or his tormentor?

» How would you explain the last line of the poem?

THE LAST SPIN

ABOUT THE AUTHOR

EVAN HUNTER

Born Salvatore Albert Lombino, Evan Hunter's (a.k.a. Ed McBain) short-lived experience as a high school teacher was the inspiration for his first successful book, *The Blackboard Jungle*. It was so successful as a book, that it was later made into a movie.

BORN October 15, 1926, in New York, N.Y.

QUOTE "I would like to win the Pulitzer Prize. I would like to win the Nobel Prize. I would like to win a Tony award for the Broadway musical I'm now working on. Aside from these, my aspirations are modest ones."

MORE ABOUT EVAN HUNTER

- His career spans over fifty years and includes novels, short stories and screenplays, with Alfred Hitchcock's *The Birds* as one of his most famous works.
- He authored the *87th Precinct* crime book series, possibly the longest, most varied and popular series in the world.
- His first professional short story was a sci-fi story called *Welcome Martians* published in 1951.
- It is believed that his pseudonym Evan Hunter is derived from the names of two schools he attended: Evander Childs High School and Hunter College.

RECOGNITIONS INCLUDE:

- He was the first American to receive the British Crime Writers Association's highest recognition: the Diamond Dagger Award in 1998.
- In 1986, he received the Grand Master Award from the Mystery Writers of America.

OTHER WORKS:

- *Cop Hater*
- *The Mugger*
- *The Pusher*
- *The Con Man*
- *Killer's Choice*
- *Killer's Payoff*
- *Killer's Wedge*
- *Lady Killer*
- *'Til Death*
- *King's Ransom*

- *The Blackboard Jungle*
- *Strangers When We Meet*
- *A Matter of Conviction*
- *Mothers and Daughters*
- *Buddwing*
- *The Paper Dragon*
- *A Horse's Head*
- *Last Summer*
- *Sons*
- *Nobody Knew They Were There*

STORY SET-UP ...

In Chapter 4, you read that someone or something might influence some of your decisions. Sometimes, even when you know you're being controlled by someone else, you don't have much choice but to comply. The following story talks about two teenage boys' adventure in gang conflict resolution. Read on to find out what may happen when control and manipulation spiral out of control.

A Before Reading

ACTIVITY 1

» Select the correct meaning for the bolded words.

1. [...] he wore a green **silk** jacket with an orange stripe on each sleeve.

   a) type of liquid   b) type of fabric   c) type of paint

2. [...] its sawed-off, two-inch barrel abruptly terminating the otherwise **lethal** grace of the weapon.

   a) deadly   b) respects the law   c) strange

3. He was nervous and **apprehensive**, but he kept tight control of his face.

   a) understanding   b) young   c) fearful

4. Tigo would not turkey out of this particular **rumble**.

   a) game   b) fall   c) fight

5. Alongside the gun were three .38 Special **cartridges**.

   a) casings for bullets   b) movies   c) precious jewels

6. [He] then snapped the gun shut and **twirled** the cylinder.

   a) bent   b) closed   c) spun

7. [...] he dried his palms on his **trousers**.

   a) hair   b) shoes   c) pants

8. [...] his sudden enthusiasm seemed to **ebb** completely.

   a) recede   b) fry   c) scream

9. Tigo looked **puzzled**.

   a) hungry   b) confused   c) handsome

ACTIVITY 2

❯ Read the following statements and decide where you stand on a scale of 1 (completely agree) to 5 (completely disagree). Be ready to defend your point of view with your classmates.

- People who join gangs usually have no other choice.

- Making a new friend is easy.

- People let themselves get manipulated.

- Loyalty is recognized and compensated.

- Poverty leads to crime.

ACTIVITY 3

❯ How do teenagers resolve conflicts? With a partner, discuss what possible conflicts teens face with other teens and how they usually get resolved. What other solutions can you think of for each conflict?

B During Reading

❯ Draw a chart to help you complete the following information about Danny and Tigo as you read:

Danny	Tigo
their approximate age	
their jacket colours	
whether they have siblings	
who has a girlfriend	
their opinion of their clubs	

❯ As you read, take notes on the subtle gestures of friendship the boys make towards each other. Identify the passages that show this.

THE LAST SPIN

BY EVAN HUNTER

The boy sitting opposite him was his enemy.

The boy sitting opposite him was called Tigo, and he wore a green silk jacket with an orange stripe on each sleeve. The jacket told Danny that Tigo was his enemy. The jacket shrieked, "Enemy, enemy!"

005> "This is a good piece," Tigo said, indicating the gun on the table. "This runs you close to forty-five bucks, you try to buy it in a store. That's a lot of money."

The gun on the table was a Smith & Wesson .38 Police Special.

It rested exactly in the center of the table, its sawed-off, two-inch barrel 010> **abruptly** terminating the otherwise lethal grace of the weapon. There was a checked walnut **stock** on the gun, and the gun was finished in a flat blue. Alongside the gun were three .38 Special cartridges.

Danny looked at the gun disinterestedly. He was nervous and apprehensive, but he kept tight control of his face. He could not show Tigo 015> what he was feeling. Tigo was the enemy, and so he presented a mask to the enemy, **cocking** one eyebrow and saying, "I seen pieces before. There's nothing special about this one." "Except what we got to do with it," Tigo said. Tigo was studying him with large brown eyes. The eyes were moist-looking. He was not a bad-looking kid, Tigo, with thick 020> black hair and maybe a nose that was too long, but his mouth and chin were good. You could usually tell a cat by his mouth and his chin. Tigo would not **turkey out** of this particular rumble. Of that, Danny was sure.

"Why don't we start?" Danny asked. He wet his lips and looked across 025> at Tigo.

"You understand," Tigo said, "I got no bad blood for you." "I understand."

"This is what the club said. This is how the club said we should settle it.

Without a big street diddlebop, *you dig*? But I want you to know
I *don't know you from a hole in the wall* – except you wear a blue
030> and gold jacket."

"And you wear a green and orange one," Danny said, "and that's enough
for me."

"Sure, but what I was trying to say …"

"We going to sit and talk all night, or we going to get this thing
035> rolling?" Danny asked.

"What I'm tryin to say," Tigo went on, "is that I just happened to
be picked for this, you know? Like to settle this thing that's between
the two clubs I mean, you got to admit your boys shouldn't have
come in our territory last night."

040>"I got to admit nothing," Danny said flatly.

"Well, anyway, they shot at the candy store. That wasn't right.
There's supposed to be a *truce* on."

"Okay, okay," Danny said.

"So like … like this is the way we agreed
045> to settle it. I mean, one of us and … and
one of you. Fair and square. Without
any street boppin', and without any
law trouble."

"Let's get on with it," Danny said.

050>"I'm trying to say, I never even seen you
on the street before this. So this ain't
nothin' personal with me. Whichever
way it turns out, like …"

"I never seen you neither," Danny said.

055> Tigo stared at him for a long time.
"That's cause you're new around here.
Where you from originally?"

Glossary

abruptly: suddenly;
all at once
stock: a handle
cocking: to turn up
turkey out: (slang) to not
do something out of fear
you dig: (slang) you
understand
**don't know you from
a hole in the wall:** (slang)
never met you before
truce: temporary end
of fighting

"My people come down from the Bronx."

"You got a big family?"

060> "A sister and two brothers, that's all."

"Yeah, I only got a sister." Tigo shrugged. "Well." He sighed. "So." He sighed again. "Let's make it, huh?"

"I'm waitin'," Danny said.

"Tigo picked up the gun, and then he took one of the cartridges
065> from the table top. He broke open the gun, slid the cartridge into the cylinder, and then snapped the gun shut and twirled the cylinder.

"Round and round she goes," he said, "and where she stops, nobody knows. There's six chambers in the cylinder and only one cartridge. That makes the odds five-to-one that the cartridge'll be in firing
070> position when the cylinder stops *whirling*. You dig?"

"I dig."

"I'll go first," Tigo said.

Danny looked at him suspiciously. "Why?"

"You want to go first?"

075> "I don't know."

"I'm giving you a break." Tigo grinned. "I may blow my head off first time out."

"Why you giving me a break?" Danny asked.

Tigo *shrugged*. "What's the difference?" He gave the cylinder
080> a fast twirl.

"The Russians invented this, huh?" Danny asked.

"Yeah."

"I always said they was crazy."

"Yeah, I always ..." Tigo stopped talking. The cylinder was stopped
085> now. He took a deep breath, put the barrel of the .38 to his temple, and then squeezed the trigger.

The firing pin clicked on an empty chamber.

"Well, that was easy, wasn't it?" he asked. He shoved the gun across the table. "Your turn, Danny."

090> Danny reached for the gun. It was cold in the basement room, but he was sweating now. He pulled the gun toward him, then left it on the table while he dried his palms on his trousers. He picked up the gun then and stared at it.

"It's a nifty piece," Tigo said. "I like a good piece."

095> "Yeah, I do too," Danny said. "You can tell a good piece just by the way it feels in your hand."

Tigo looked surprised. "I mentioned that to one of the guys yesterday, and he thought I was nuts."

"Lots of guys don't know about pieces," Danny said, shrugging. "I was
100> thinking," Tigo said, "when I get old enough, I'll join the Army, you know? I'd like to work around pieces."

"I thought of that, too. I'd join now only my *old lady* won't give me permission. She's got to sign if I join now."

"Yeah, they're all the same," Tigo said smiling. "Your old lady born
105> here or the old country?"

"The old country," Danny said.

"Yeah, well you know they got these old-fashioned ideas."

"I better spin," Danny said.

"Yeah," Tigo agreed.

110> Danny slapped the cylinder with his left hand. The cylinder whirled, whirled, and then stopped. Slowly, Danny put the gun to his head. He wanted to close his eyes, but he didn't dare. Tigo, the enemy, was watching him. He returned Tigo's stare,
115> and then he squeezed the trigger.

Glossary

whirling: spinning around
shrugged: raised the shoulders
old lady: (slang) mother

His heart skipped a beat, and then over the roar of his blood he heard the empty click. **Hastily**, he put the gun down on the table.

"Makes you sweat, don't it?" Tigo said.

120> Danny nodded, saying nothing. He watched Tigo. Tigo was looking at the gun.

"Me now, huh?" Tigo said. He took a deep breath, then picked up the .38. He twirled the cylinder, waited for it to stop, and then put the gun to his head.

"Bang!" Tigo said, and then he squeezed the trigger. Again the firing
125> pin clicked on an empty chamber. Tigo let out his breath and put the gun down.

"I thought I was dead that time," he said.

"I could hear the **harps**," Danny said.

"My old lady's like a house," Danny said laughing. "She ought to try
130> this kind of a diet." He laughed at his own humor, pleased when Tigo joined him.

"That's the trouble," Tigo said. "You see a nice deb in the street, you think it's crazy, you know? Then they get to be our people's age, and they turn to fat." He shook his head.

135>"You got a chick?" Danny asked.

"Yeah, I got one."

"What's her name?"

"Aw, you don't know her."

"Maybe I do," Danny said.

140>"Her name is Juana." Tigo watched him. "She's about five-two, got these brown eyes …"

"I think I know her," Danny said. He nodded. "Yeah, I think I know her."

"She's nice, ain't she?" Tigo asked. He leaned forward, as if Danny's
145> answer was of great importance to him.

"Yeah she's nice," Danny said.

"Yeah. Hey maybe sometime we could …" Tigo cut himself short. He looked down at the gun, and his sudden enthusiasm seemed to ebb completely. "It's your turn," he said.

150> "Here goes nothing," Danny said. He twirled the cylinder, sucked in his breath, and then fired.

The emptily click was loud in the stillness of the room.

"Man!" Danny said.

"We're pretty lucky, you know?" Tigo said.

155> "So far."

"We better lower the odds. The boys won't like it if we …" He stopped himself again, and then reached for one of the cartridges on the table. He broke open the gun again, slipped in the second cartridge into the cylinder. "Now we got two cartridges in here," he said. "Two cartridges, 160> six chambers. That's four-to-two. Divide it, and you get two-to-two." He paused. "You game?"

"That's … that's what we're here for, ain't it?"

"Sure."

"Okay then."

165> "Gone," Tigo said, nodding his head. "You got courage, Danny."

"You're the one needs the courage," Danny said gently. "It's your spin."

Tigo lifted the gun. Idly, he began spinning the cylinder.

"You live on the next block, don't you?" Danny asked.

"Yeah." Tigo kept slapping the cylinder.

170> It spun with a gently whirring sound.

"That's how come we never crossed paths, I guess. Also, I'm new on the scene."

"Yeah, well you know, you get hooked up with one club, that's the way it is."

Glossary

Hastily: quickly
harps: musical instrument said to be played by angels

175> "You like the guys on your club?" Danny asked, wondering why he was asking such a stupid question, listening to the whirring of the cylinder at the same time.

"They're okay." Tigo shrugged. "None of them really send me, but that's the club on my block, so what're you gonna do, huh?" His hand left
180> the cylinder. It stopped spinning. He put the gun to his head.

"Wait!" Danny said.

Tigo looked puzzled. "What's the matter?"

"Nothing. I just wanted to say … I mean …" Danny frowned. "I don't dig too many of the guys on my club, either."

185> Tigo nodded. For a moment, their eyes locked. Then Tigo shrugged, and fired.

The empty click filled the basement room.

"Phew," Tigo said.

"Man, you can say that again."

190> Tigo slid the gun across the table.

Danny hesitated an instant. He did not want to pick up the gun. He felt sure that this time the firing pin would strike the percussion cap of one of the cartridges. He was sure that this time he would shoot himself.

195> "Sometimes I think I'm turkey," he said to Tigo, surprised that his thoughts had found voice.

"I feel that way sometimes, too," Tigo said.

"I never told that to nobody," Danny said. "The guys on my club would laugh at me, I ever told them that."

200> "Some things you got to keep to yourself. There ain't nobody you can trust in this world."

"There should be somebody you can trust," Danny said. "Hell, you can't tell nothing to your people. They don't understand." Tigo laughed. "That's an old story. But that's the way things are.
205> What're you gonna do?"

"Yeah. Still, sometimes I think I'm turkey."

"Sure, sure," Tigo said. "It ain't only that, though. Like sometimes … well, don't you wonder what you're doing stomping some guy in the street? Like … you know what I mean? Like … who's the guy to you?
210> What you got to beat him up for? 'Cause he messed with somebody else's girl?" Tigo shook his head. "It gets complicated sometimes."

"Yeah, but …" Danny frowned again. "You got to stick with the club. Don't you?"

"Sure, sure … yeah." Again, their eyes locked.

215> "Well, here goes." Danny said. He lifted the gun. "It's just …" He shook his head, and then twirled the cylinder. The cylinder spun, and then stopped. He studied the gun, wondering if one of the cartridges would roar from the barrel when he squeezed the trigger.

Then he fired.

220> Click.

"I didn't think you was going through with it," Tigo said.

"I didn't neither."

"You got heart, Danny," Tigo said. He looked at the gun. He picked it up and broke it open.

225> "What you doing?" Danny asked.

"Another cartridge," Tigo said. "Six chambers, three cartridges. That makes it even money. You game?"

"You?" "The boys said … " Tigo stopped talking. "Yeah, I'm game," he added, his voice curiously low.

230> "It's your turn, you know."

"I know," Danny watched as Tigo picked up the gun.

"You ever been rowboating on the lake?"

Tigo looked across the table at Danny, his eyes wide. "Once," he said. "I went with Juana."

235> "Is it … is it any kicks?"

"Yeah. Yeah, its grand kicks. You mean you never been?"

"No," Danny said.

"Hey, you got to try it, man," Tigo said excitedly. "You'll like it. Hey, you try it."

240> "Yeah, I was thinking maybe this Sunday I'd ... " He did not complete the sentence.

"My spin," Tigo said wearily. He twirled the cylinder. "Here goes a good man," he said, and he put the revolver to his head and squeezed the trigger.

245> Click.

Danny smiled nervously. "No rest for the *weary*," he said. "But man you've got the heart. I don't know if I can go through with it."

"Sure, you can," Tigo assured him. "Listen, what's there to be afraid of?" He slid the gun across the table.

250> "We keep this up all night?" Danny asked.

"They said ... you know ... "

"Well, it ain't so bad. I mean, if we didn't have this operation, we wouldn'ta got a chance to talk, huh?" He grinned feebly.

"Yeah," Tigo said, his face splitting in a wide grin.

255> "It ain't been so bad, huh?"

"No, it's been … well, you know, these guys on the club, who can talk to them?"

He picked up the gun. "We could …" Tigo started.

"What?"

260> "We could say … well … like we kept shootin' an' nothing happened, so …" Tigo shrugged. "We can't do this all night, can we?"

"I don't know."

"Let's make this the last spin. Listen, they don't like it, they can take a flying leap, you know?"

265> "I don't think they'll like it. We're supposed to settle this for the clubs."

"Forget about the clubs!" Tigo said. "Can't we pick our own …" The word was hard coming. When it came, his eyes did not leave Danny's face. "… friends?"

"Sure we can," Danny said **vehemently**. "Sure we can! Why not?"

270> "The last spin," Tigo said. "Come on, the last spin."

"Gone," Danny said. "Hey you know, I'm glad they got this idea. You know that? I'm actually glad!" He twirled the cylinder. "Look, you want to go on the lake this Sunday? I mean with your girl and mine? We could get two boats. Or even one if you want." "Yeah, one boat,"

275> Tigo said. "Hey, your girl'll like Juana, I mean it. She's a swell chick."

The cylinder stopped. Danny put the gun to his head quickly.

"Here's to Sunday," he said. He grinned at Tigo, and Tigo grinned back, and then Danny fired.

The explosion rocked the small
280> basement room, ripping away half of Danny's head, shattering his face. A small cry escaped Tigo's throat, and a look of incredulous shock **knifed his eyes**. Then he put his head on the table
285> and began weeping.

Glossary

weary: tired
vehemently: forcefully
knifed his eyes: imagery meaning flashed in his eyes

After Reading

ACTIVITY 1

» Reread the story to the end of line 54.

1. Explain the significance of the boys' jackets.

2. What event caused this encounter?

3. What other option did the gangs consider to settle the dispute?

» Now reread lines 55 to 190.

4. '"I could hear the harps," Danny said.' What does he mean by that?

5. How does Tigo make the game more dangerous?

6. "Tigo looked puzzled." (line 182) Why?

» Finally, reread from line 191 to the end of the story.

7. "Yeah, I was thinking that maybe this Sunday I'd ... " He did not complete the sentence. Why?

8. Why did Tigo weep when his "enemy" died?

9. Tigo and Danny learn more and more about each other as the story progresses. Their friendship develops when they realize they have many common interests, thoughts and opinions. Make a list of everything they have in common.

10. Which boy seems the more nervous and scared of the two? What passage(s) indicate(s) this?

ACTIVITY 2

» Based on what you now know of Tigo and Danny, how do you think they would have completed the following sentences taken directly from the text?

1. Tigo: "Yeah. Hey maybe sometime we could …" (line 147)

2. Tigo: "We better lower the odds. The boys won't like it if we …" (line 156)

3. Tigo: "The boys said …" (line 228)

4. Danny: "Yeah, I was thinking maybe this Sunday I'd …" (line 240)

5. Tigo: "We could …" (line 258)

ACTIVITY 3

» Based on the context, replace the underlined slang terms with a word that means the same.

1. "Without a big street diddlebop, you dig?" (line 28)

2. "I'd join now only my old lady won't give me permission." (line 102)

3. "Sometimes I think I'm turkey." (line 195)

4. "Is it … is it any kicks?" (line 235)

» Why do you think Danny and Tigo use slang terms when talking?

D Comparing the Two Stories

» Answer the following questions for each of the three boys (Dickie, Danny and Tigo) from *Examination Day* and *The Last Spin*. You may draw a chart to enter your answers.

1. Who is controlling them?

2. What kind of relationship do they have with their parents?

3. What was each boy's tragic ending?

» Both stories end tragically. What could each boy have done to prevent his fate?

E Your Thoughts?

1. '"You understand," Tigo said, "I got no bad blood for you."' Why do you think the author includes this statement from Tigo early in the story?

2. Do you think Tigo will go back to his club after Danny's death, or will he leave the club and begin a new life? Why?

3. Both Tigo and Danny had the opportunity to simply take the gun and shoot the other. Why do you think neither did that?

4. Do you think it's possible for two people to become friends in such a short period of time? Explain why, based on your life experiences.

5. How do you think the clubs would have reacted if Danny and Tigo had both survived and decided to stay friends?

6. Do you think Danny or Tigo could have safely left their gangs and started a new life (before their encounter)? Why?

F Links to Chapter 4

1. The notion of control is present throughout the story. Do the two boys know they're being controlled? Explain.

2. At what point in the story do Danny and Tigo try to regain control of their destinies? How do they do so?

3. Are teenagers easier to manipulate than adults? Explain.

4. a) In your opinion, what life decisions did Danny and Tigo make that led them to a life in gangs?

   b) Who do you believe influenced their decisions?

THE KISS

KATE CHOPIN

Born Katherine O'Flaherty, she was an American writer of short stories and novels. At 19, she started writing stories in magazines and newspapers. Although she was discouraged by criticism and never made much money from her writing, she has been recognized as one of the most influential writers of her time. She is also considered to be a forerunner of 20th century feminist authors.

BORN February 8, 1850 in St. Louis, Missouri.

QUOTE "And moreover, to succeed, the artist must possess the courageous soul … the brave soul. The soul that dares and defies."

MORE ABOUT KATE CHOPIN

- Much of her inspiration comes from when she lived in Louisiana near a cotton plantation, especially from the Creole culture of the area.
- Her second novel, *The Awakening*, published in 1899, was greatly criticized because of moral issues and literary standards. It is the story of a woman oppressed by society.
- Discouraged by criticism, she went back to writing short stories.
- She depended mostly on her investments in St. Louis to sustain her.
- Ten years after her death, she was considered as one of the leading writers of her time. Some even described her as having a native aptitude for narration amounting almost to genius.

RECOGNITIONS INCLUDE:

- She received honourary degrees from both Yale and Oxford universities.
- She was admitted to the American Academy of Arts and Letters in 1904.

OTHER WORKS:

- *At Fault*
- *The Awakening*
- *Bayou Folk*
- *A Night In Acadie*
- *The Storm*
- *The Story of an Hour*
- *Désirée's Baby*

- *A Pair of Silk Stockings*
- *Athénaïse*
- *At the 'Cadian Ball*
- *Lilacs*
- *A Respectable Woman*
- *The Unexpected*
- *A Very Fine Fiddle*

STORY SET-UP ...

In Chapter 5, you thought about and defined the ideal life. In this story, you will read about how a woman's idea of the perfect life involves wealth, status, love and passion. She is quite determined to achieve all this, even if it takes two men! Her perfect plan, however, may take an unexpected turn, as is often the case with affairs of the heart.

A Before Reading

ACTIVITY 1

❯ Match the words in the box below to their definition.

WORD Bank

smouldering	blustering	sought	lingering
clutching	guile	stride	mingled

1. Another name for a very long step

2. The past participle of to seek

3. An adjective meaning to be loud

4. Burning without a flame

5. To be mixed with something else

6. Grasping tightly with your hand

7. Skill to achieve your goals through subtle means

8. To be slow in quitting or leaving something

ACTIVITY 2

❯ In the story you are about to read, the main character will face the repercussions of a dilemma. In preparation for reading, answer the following questions. Discuss your answers with a partner.

a) For an important decision, should you follow your heart or your head?

b) What do you think are the outcomes of lying to yourself?

c) In which situations can reason interfere with your emotions?

ACTIVITY 3

Using resources, find the meaning of the expression "You can't have your cake and eat it too."

a) Explain the expression using your own words.

b) Describe a time when you wanted to have your cake and eat it too.

c) Based on this expression and the Story Set-Up, predict what you think this story will be about.

B During Reading

ACTIVITY 1

❂ Brantain and Nathalie have different feelings toward each other. As you read, take notes on character details that show how one perceives the other.

Your answers may take this form:

Examples:

 – Nathalie is … because she …

 – Brantain is … because he …

❂ Note a sentence from the text that describes each character's disposition toward the other.

ACTIVITY 2

❂ This story takes place well over one hundred years ago. Look for clues in the text that indicate this. Add these clues to your notes as you read. The clues may be found in:

 – the characters' actions, habits or speech

 – the surroundings or environment

 – the vocabulary the author uses

THE KISS

BY KATE CHOPIN

It was still daylight outside, but inside with the curtains drawn and the smouldering fire sending out a dim, uncertain glow, the room was full of deep shadows.

Brantain sat in one of these shadows; it had **overtaken** him and he did
005> not mind. The obscurity gave him courage to keep his eyes focused as much as he liked upon the girl who sat in the firelight.

She was very handsome, with a certain fine, rich coloring that belongs to the healthy brune type. She was quite **composed**, as she gently stroked the soft fur of the cat that lay curled in her lap, and she occasionally
010> sent a slow glance into the shadow where her companion sat. They were talking low, of indifferent things which clearly were not the things that occupied their thoughts. She knew that he loved her—a frank, blustering fellow without guile enough to hide his feelings, and no desire to do so. For the last two weeks, he had eagerly and persistently
015> spent time with her. She was confidently waiting for him to declare himself and she meant to accept him. The rather insignificant and unattractive Brantain was enormously rich; and she liked and required the entourage which wealth could give her.

During one of the pauses between their talk of the last tea and the next
020> reception, the door opened and a young man entered whom Brantain knew quite well. The girl turned her face toward him. A stride or two brought him to her side, and bending over her chair—before she could suspect his intention, for she did not realize that he had not seen her visitor—he pressed an ardent, lingering kiss upon her lips.

025> Brantain slowly arose; so did the girl arise, but quickly, and the newcomer stood between them, a little amusement and some defiance mixed with the confusion in his face.

"I believe," **stammered** Brantain, "I see that I have stayed too long. I—
I had no idea—that is, I must wish you good-by." He was clutching his
030> hat with both hands, and probably did not realize that she was extending
her hand to him, her sense of reasoning had not completely abandoned
her; but she could not have trusted herself to speak.

"Hang me if I saw him sitting there, Nattie! I know it's **deuced awkward**
for you. But I hope you'll forgive me this once—this very first break.
035> Why, what's the matter?"

"Don't touch me; don't come near me," she returned angrily. "What
do you mean by entering the house without ringing?"

"I came in with your brother, as I often do," he answered coldly, in
self-justification. "We came in the side way. He went upstairs and
040> I came in here hoping to find you. The explanation is simple enough
and should satisfy you that the misadventure was inevitable. But do
say that you forgive me, Nathalie," he **entreated**, softening.

"Forgive you! You don't know what you are talking about. Let me pass.
It depends upon—a good deal whether I ever forgive you."

045> At that next reception which she and Brantain had been talking
about, she approached the young man
with a delicious directness and honesty
when she saw him there.

"Will you let me speak to you a moment
050> or two, Mr. Brantain?" she asked with
an engaging but perturbed smile.
He seemed extremely unhappy; but
when she took his arm and walked
away with him, seeking a quiet corner,
055> a ray of hope mingled with the almost
comical misery of his expression.
She was apparently very **outspoken**.

Glossary

overtaken: caught up with
composed: calm
stammered: spoke with
hesitation
deuced: (informally used
to stress a point) darned;
blasted
awkward: embarrassing
entreated: pleaded
outspoken: direct in her
speech

"Perhaps I should not have sought this interview, Mr. Brantain; but—but, oh, I have been very uncomfortable, almost miserable since that little
060> encounter the other afternoon. When I thought how you might have misinterpreted it, and believed things" —hope was clearly conquering the misery in Brantain's round, guileless face— "Of course, I know it is nothing to you, but for my own sake I do want you to understand that Mr. Harvy is a long-time intimate friend. Why, we have always
065> been like cousins—like brother and sister, I may say. He is my brother's most intimate associate and often believes that he is entitled to the same privileges as the family. Oh, I know it is absurd, **uncalled for**, to tell you this; undignified even," she was almost **weeping**, "but it makes so much difference to me what you think of—of me." Her voice had
070> grown very low and agitated. The misery had all disappeared from Brantain's face.

"Then you do really care what I think, Miss Nathalie? May I call you Miss Nathalie?" They turned into a long, dim corridor that was lined on either side with tall, graceful plants. They walked slowly to the very
075> end of it. When they turned to retrace their steps Brantain's face was **radiant** and hers was triumphant.

***

Harvy was among the guests at the wedding; and he sought her out in a rare moment when she stood alone.

"Your husband," he said, smiling, "has sent me over to kiss you."

080> A quick **blush** filled her face and round polished throat. "I suppose it's natural for a man to feel and act generously on an occasion of this kind. He tells me he doesn't want his marriage to interrupt that pleasant intimacy which has existed between you and me. I don't know what you've been telling him," with an insolent smile, "but
085> he has sent me here to kiss you."

She felt like a chess player who, by the clever handling of his pieces, sees the game taking the course intended. Her eyes were bright and tender with a smile as they glanced up into his; and her lips looked hungry for the kiss which they invited.

090> "But, you know," he went on quietly, "I didn't tell him so, it would have seemed ungrateful, but I can tell you. I've stopped kissing women; it's dangerous."

Well, she had Brantain and his million left. A person can't have everything in this world; and it was a little unreasonable of her
095> to expect it.

Glossary

uncalled for: not required
weeping: crying
radiant: reflecting happiness
blush: a rosy colour

C After Reading

ACTIVITY 1

❯ Find all the passages in the text that indicate to the reader that Nathalie is interested in both men. You may make a chart to help you.

Example of a chart:

Brantain	Harvy
Passage 1	Passage 1

ACTIVITY 2

❯ Reread the story to the end of line 18.

a) Why did the obscurity give Brantain courage to stare at Nathalie?

b) What line indicates that Nathalie is only vaguely interested in her companion?

c) What attracted Nathalie to Brantain?

❯ Now reread lines 19 to 57.

d) When Harvy entered, how do you know he had not seen Brantain sitting in the obscurity?

e) Name two physical reactions that show Brantain is upset by the kiss.

f) How do you know this is not the first time Harvy visits Nathalie at her house?

g) How does Brantain feel when Nathalie approaches him at the reception?

⊙ Finally, reread from line 58 to the end of the story.

h) How does Nathalie justify her kiss with Harvy?

i) What is the first indication that Brantain has forgiven Nathalie?

j) What gesture confirms that Brantain believed Nathalie's lie about her relationship with Harvy?

k) "She felt like a chess player who, by the clever handling of his pieces, sees the game taking the course intended." (line 86) Describe what intended course the author is referring to.

l) Why does Harvy tell Nathalie that he's "stopped kissing women; it's dangerous." (line 91)?

D Your Thoughts?

1. How would you have reacted if you were Brantain when Harvy walked in and kissed Nathalie?

2. Do you believe Nathalie was justified in getting angry at Harvy when he kissed her? Why?

3. Even though Harvy explains how he's done nothing wrong, he nonetheless apologizes to Nathalie. Why does he do this?

4. Why do you think Nathalie is so intent on winning back Brantain?

5. Why do you think she feels like a chess player at the end of the story?

6. Do you believe Nathalie wanted to "have her cake and eat it too"? Why?

7. How would you describe Nathalie's personality? Why?

8. Knowing this story takes place over a century ago, do you believe something like this can still happen today?

E Links to Chapter 5

1. In Chapter 5, you dealt with the concept of perfection. What do you think is Nathalie's idea of a perfect life?

2. a) Explain why Nathalie's plan for a perfect life didn't come to pass.

   b) Do you believe she can still achieve her "perfect" life? Why?

3. How realistic are Nathalie's expectations of a perfect life? Why?